Advance Praise for *A Daily Spiritual Rx*

Anyone who has genuinely benefited from the reading of spiritual classics will know that the key to their value lies not in being able to say that they have been read, but in being able to say that some measure of their content has been experienced and woven into the fabric of their lives. Joanna Seibert offers a rich introduction to that literature which makes it possible to begin that journey. Whether one reads and prays with the selections on offer here or presses further into the contributions that each writer makes, this compendium will be a valuable companion. I can recommend it wholeheartedly.

> The Rev. Dr. Frederick W. Schmidt
> Rueben P. Job Chair in Spiritual Formation
> Garrett-Evangelical Theological Seminary, Evanston, Illinois

"As iron sharpens iron, so one person's wit sharpens another." Prov. 27:17. There's definitely a lot of iron in the quotations selected for this daily reader by Joanna Seibert, great depth as well as breadth from folks like Richard Rohr, Henry Nouwen, Barbara Taylor and Steven Charleston to name a few. But the real strength of this book comes from the author's own reflections as she responds to the other voices. It's when she lets the iron of her own life be sharpened by others, that the sparks really begin to fly. I'm looking forward to the Rev. Dr. Seibert's book beginning this Lent and Easter, but the medicine in it can be taken at any time.

> The Rev. Danny Schieffler
> Rector of St. Mark's Episcopal Church, Little Rock, Arkansas

When I started reading this book I did not want to stop. Dr. Joanna Seibert knows the limits of human understanding: "I still have no answers for how to handle the death of a child," she admits. She makes no pretense of heroic virtue: "I wish that I was able to write that I went out and planted trees, but alas my kitchen floor was as far as I got," she confesses, writing about the first Earth Day in 1970—when she was pregnant, and stripping floor wax, and her husband was packing for a year in Vietnam. Through all of that and in every nook and cranny, God is in this book.

> The Rev. Dr. Chris Keller
> Dean, Trinity Cathedral, Little Rock, Arkansas

Spiritual directors walk with us along our path. They don't tell us which road to take. Instead, they help us encounter God along the way that we are actually taking. In her book *A Spiritual Rx for Lent and Easter*, Joanna Seibert displays her exquisite gifts as a spiritual friend. The book's brief excerpts from well-known spiritual writers and Joanna's own insightful reflections invite us to look for the divine in the contours of our ordinary lives. If you're looking for a richer experience of the holy in your life, Joanna Seibert has written the right prescription (Rx) for you.

> The Right Rev. Jake Owensby
> Bishop of the Episcopal Church in Western Louisiana
> Author of *A Resurrection Shaped Life: Dying and Rising on Planet Earth*

Joanna Seibert quotes Alan Jones within these pages, "The opposite of faith is not doubt, but certainty." Religion is at its best not when it provides pat answers, but when it asks deep questions, encouraging us along the spiritual journey. In *A Daily Spiritual Rx*, Joanna Seibert poses, again and again, questions that paradoxically provoke and comfort at the same time. Joanna journeys with us through Lent and Easter, introducing us to the ideas of sages and saints, and she gives us a glimpse into the deep wisdom of her own experience as a deacon, a physician and a spiritual director. This book will not satiate you. It will do something better than that: It will stoke your hunger to know God and be your companion as you walk the pilgrim way from Ash Wednesday to the Resurrection.

> The Very Reverend Barkley Thompson
> Dean, Christ Church Cathedral Houston, Texas
> Author of *Elements of Grace* and *In the Midst of the City: The Gospel and God's Politics*

A Daily Spiritual Rx
for Lent and Easter

Su
Bless you on you
day through Lint t
Easter

Joanna J. Seibert

Other books by Joanna Seibert

Earth Songs Press (Imprint: Temenos Publishing)

Healing Presence

The Call of the Psalms: A Spiritual Companion for Busy People

The Call of the Psalms: A Spiritual Companion for People in Recovery

Taste and See

Blessed Hope

Interpreting the World to the Church Vol. 1: Sermons for the Church Year

Interpreting the World to the Church Vol. 2: Sermons for Special Times

A Daily Spiritual Rx
for Lent and Easter

Joanna J. Seibert

EARTH SONGS PRESS

earthsongspress.com

Earth Songs Press

A DAILY SPIRITUAL RX FOR LENT AND EASTER

Library of Congress Cataloging-in-Publication-Data has been applied for.

Cover Art:
"Icon of St. Joanna the Myrrh-Bearer"
Uncut Mountain Supply
www.uncutmountainsupply.com

Proceeds from *A Daily Spiritual Rx for Lent and Easter* will be donated to Hurricane Relief in the Central Gulf Coast.

Printed in the United States of America
ISBN 978-0-578-42513-9

earthsongspress.com

To the faithful people at the churches where I have served as a deacon: St. Margaret's, St. Mark's, and Trinity Cathedral Little Rock, St. Luke's North Little Rock and Holy Spirit, Gulf Shores Alabama; to the faithful followers of my daily blog the *Daily Something* at joannaseibert.com who share with me your thoughts about what I write; and to the followers of my blog on Facebook. Your words have enriched my life of words and taught me about the powerful presence of God in community.

An established author with over forty years of experience as a physician, minister, mother, retreat leader, and spiritual director, Joanna has collected daily messages from well-known spiritual authors and responds with a short discussion from her own experience as it relates to spiritual direction. *A Daily Spiritual Rx* should trigger a connection to God for the reader from her own experience to sustain her for the day. Joanna addresses the most common subjects and questions brought up by people on spiritual journeys or in spiritual direction as she shares books, readings, and experiences that have most connected her to God on her journey from both contemporary and classical writers.

Joanna is a frequent and well-known retreat leader and the multiple readings on varying subjects in the book are an excellent way to journey with readers on a retreat. The book could be part of curriculum in spiritual direction classes and schools, men's and women's church groups, pastoral care classes and schools. It also speaks to those in 12-step recovery groups. Special writings address the liturgical seasons of Lent, Holy Week, and Easter.

Contents

Lent: Ash Wednesday

Buechner: Lent Ash Wednesday

"In many cultures there is an ancient custom of giving a tenth of each year's income to some holy use. For Christians, to observe the forty days of Lent is to do the same thing with roughly a tenth of each year's days."

–Frederick Buechner, *Whistling in the Dark: An ABC Theologized.* Harper Collins, 2009.

We begin our Lenten journey on this Ash Wednesday. It is a day to remember our mortality, "dust you are and to dust you shall return." I think of my favorite aunt who had Alzheimer's for over ten years who died today on Ash Wednesday.

I watch the members of our parish receive the imposition of ashes. Some have cancer or are ill, and I know well they worry whether they will be present in this body at this church next Ash Wednesday. Some are filled with tears at the altar. I wonder who will meet death face to face before next Easter. Could it be even myself or a member of my family?

I travel in time back to the Cathedral School where I remember comments from the elementary students as we placed ashes on their foreheads. "Will it stay on? How do I look? You look funny." Now a beautiful young mother holding her three-month old baby girl comes up to the altar. Our priest puts the sign of the cross on the mother's forehead. I do not want her to put the cross on this baby's head. I watch as she asks the mother and then puts the black ashes on the tiny forehead. The little girl does not cry out, but I want to stand up and cry, "No, don't do that!" My life profession has been to take care of small babies. I do not want to think of this precious one dying. I will not permit it. I still have no answers as how to handle the death of a child.

Ash Wednesday is a reminder of our immortality. I still have difficulty with it. There is a huge part of me that lives as though I and others will live forever. Easter tells me there is more than this life, resurrection, what Barbara Crafton calls the "Also Life," but I still cling to this present moment.

I think again of my aunt. In fact, I feel her presence. A friend calls to tell me that a dear friend is having her first baby today and has asked for prayers. I pray that the spirit of my aunt will be by the bed of my friend to guide and protect her and her unborn child.

One friend dies, another is born. We all carry the blackened sign of the cross on our forehead. I return to the Cathedral School and remember a sermon by Beth Maze, "creation is made from dust."

It is good that we have these forty days to ponder all this.

Solomon and Wells: Is Love Stronger?

"Place me like a seal over your heart, like a seal on your arm; for love is as strong as death, its jealousy unyielding as the grave. It burns like blazing fire, like a mighty flame."

–Song of Solomon 8:6

Samuel Wells is the vicar at St. Martins-in-the-Fields in London and a frequent writer for *Christian Century*. He recently titled his article, "Is Love Stronger?" Wells tells the story of visiting with the husband of a wife who committed suicide whom he did not know and hearing their story, then delivering the homily at her service suggesting that all is now well. When he went to visit the husband a week later, he was met with anger about his homily. All had not been well with the woman who had a painful wasting disease and all was not well with her husband. The husband said he told Wells that before the funeral.

Wells said he learned from this experience that when being with people living with tragedy or living in the aftermath of tragedy, all he has to offer is his presence beside them. There are not words to make the situation better and attempts to clean up the situation do not affirm the difficulty they are facing. Wells believes that his role is "not to make things better for someone. It's to face the truth with them." This is what the love stronger than death is. It is presence, not words.

This is also true when we meet with spiritual friends. Trying to see God in any difficult situation often is just listening to our friend's story and letting them know that we are beside them. We are not there to make things better, but to be a loving presence beside them in a great storm. In times of great tragedy, I remember people who just came and sat beside me and cried with me. Often the person who can best do this is someone who has known a similar tragedy. This is the love stronger than death.

–Samuel Wells, "Faith Matters: Is Love Stronger?" *Christian Century*, April 25, 2018, p. 35.

Love

"Hatred stirs up strife,
but love covers all offences."

–Proverbs 10:12

We are all banking on this being true. I think of all my offences, the evil I have done, the harm I have done consciously or unconsciously, the friends, the family members I have hurt. I make amends when I can for the harm I have done, but mostly I try to make living amends. I hope to learn to love the way my granddaughter, Langley, is doing to this young child on her mission trip. I want to hold closely the Christ in others and let them know what a treasure they are. I want to be able to see the Christ in them. This is what spiritual friends do for each other. They affirm, stand by each other.

More often now I am paying it forward. For many reasons I cannot make amends to the person I have harmed, but instead I try to show the love I wish I could now give to them to someone else. Paying forward is showing love to someone else that has done nothing for us, especially someone we do not know and often someone who feels loveless.

I try, I judge, I make mistakes, I mess up, I hurt others, I make amends, I try to show love that has been so often unconditionally given to me, and the cycle seems invariably to start all over again. It is a circular path. It is the human condition. I try to stay connected to this circular pathway of others who know more than I know how to love and hope to learn from them. I can so easily see Christ in them and occasionally they can see the Christ in me which guides me back onto the path of love.

Today, I now learn most about how to love from my grandchildren. What a circular life, for I first learned about love from my own grandparents many years ago.

Wounded Healer

"To be a conscious person in this world, to be aware of all the suffering and the beauty, means to have your heart broken over and over again."

–Sharon Salzberg, "Daily Quote." InwardOutward.org, May 31, 2018.

Sharon Salzberg is an author and teacher of Buddhist meditation practices. Those in Christian and psychological traditions will recognize this Buddhist belief we share as the Christian and Jungian teaching of the wounded healer. The best healers are those who also have experienced and have known the most about suffering. We daily see this in our small group grief recovery group, Walking the Mourner's Path. Three or four of us are the facilitators holding the group together. The real healers are those participating in the group who are trying to live through the death of a loved one and know something about what the others in the group are thinking and feeling. The same is true for all of those in 12-step recovery groups.

When we talk with spiritual friends who are suffering, we listen and listen and listen. At some point they will mention someone else who is suffering who helped or reached out to them. This is our clue subtlety to tell them that perhaps at some future date they can be able do the same for someone else. It is the old native American message of having walked in someone else's moccasins that gives us compassion for that person when we have a hint of what his or her life is like.

Sometimes the only resurrection that we ever see in tremendous suffering is developing an awareness of what it is like for others who are also in distress.

We have a choice, bitterness for the suffering or an understanding of compassion for others who also struggle.

Four disciplines are telling us this same message about the wounded healer. I know there must be other traditions as well who are sending this message. When several disciplines intersect, for me this is a sign of a truth.

Lent I: First Week in Lent

Praying Lectio Divina

Lectio Divina means Divine Reading. It is a prayerful way to read scripture or any spiritual writing.

Read – Read Deeply
> Read a scripture passage slowly and hear deeply the sound and meaning of every word. Imagine that God is speaking to you through these words. Listen attentively to see which word or phrase catches your attention and speaks to you and your life.

Meditate – Think, Imagine Deeply
> Take what caught your attention from your reading and think deeply about it using your imagination. Imagine what it meant to those at that time who first heard it? Why is this important to you and your tradition and your experience and your life today? What about it particularly moves you.

Pray – Pray from the Heart
> If your heart is moved or your emotions touched, go with the feelings and offer what you are feeling to God in prayer.

Contemplate – Rest
> Fall into the love of God and the love from God that was generated. Rest in the silence. Just be.

Remember – Reflect
> Journal if possible about what happened during the prayer. Memorize or copy the thought that moved you and try to remember it from time to time during the day.

–Modified from the Community of Reconciliation at Washington National Cathedral and the Friends of St. Benedict

Lectio Divina is an ancient Benedictine practice of reading the scriptures, which similar to centering prayer cultivates contemplative prayer. It was practiced in community in monasteries during the time of

St. Benedict. This is a time-honored way to try to connect to God through reading scripture, prayer, meditation, and contemplation or listening for God. If your tradition has fixed lectionary readings for Sunday, this is an excellent way to prepare for Sunday by practicing Lectio Divina with one or all of the readings daily as your personal discipline or in a group.

Macrina Wiederkehr in her book, *A Tree Full of Angels: Seeing the Holy in the Ordinary*, writes extensively about Lectio Divina, calling it "plowing up the field of the soul." She uses as her guide a quote from the Benedictine Abbot Marmion, "Read under the eye of God until your heart is touched, then give yourself up to love." She uses imagery in the process, and waits for a mantra, a holy word, a phrase, a sentence that may stay. She then carries that word or phrase with her during the day. She describes giving yourself to God as surrender, melting into God.

God's Presence

"Union with God is not something we acquire by a technique. Because God is the ground of our being, separation is impossible. God does not know how to be absent."

–Martin Laird, "Daily Quote." InwardOutward.org, May 16, 2018.

We may feel that God is not beside us or that we have been abandoned by God, but Martin Laird reminds us that God is never absent. Never absent. Never absent. We need to remind ourselves about this every day, every moment. We are never alone. The vastness of God's presence and God's love is greater than we can know or feel or imagine.

My experience is that when I start asking for more love from friends and family than they can give, this is a stop sign that I have become disconnected from God's presence. I am asking others to give more love than they can give because I do not feel God's love. When I talk to people in spiritual direction who feel estranged from God, I remind them of my experience.

So, how do we change? How do we feel God's presence and God's love rather than God's absence? My experience is that we have become disconnected especially with the Christ within us. There are a multitude of ways to try to put ourselves in position to know and feel that love of God that is always there. That is the purpose of all of the spiritual exercises. Some make gratitude lists. Some try to be more intentional about their prayer time, spending more time with God, listening instead of talking. Some spend more time in Nature where God's presence and beauty is overwhelming.

Another place we are told God is always present is among the sick, the poor, the needy, the lonely. My experience is that visiting those in need is one of the surest way to connect with the Christ in another who then reflects to us the Christ in ourselves that has been there all along. Working at a food pantry, visiting the sick, sitting with someone who is lonely is where we find God.

The paradox is that getting out of ourselves leads us back to the God within.

De Mello: Albums and Awareness

"This return to past scenes where you felt love and joy is one of the finest exercises I know for building up your psychological health."

–Anthony de Mello, *Sadhana: A Way to God*. Image Books, 1984.

I must admit that I decided to read Anthony de Mello's book, *Sadhana: A Way to God*, while I was studying about spiritual direction because it is not long, looked like easy reading, and I knew I had a great deal going on in my life in the next coming weeks of study! Well, it is only 140 pages, but it is the kind of material where one should practice one exercise one day at a time for 140 days or even better one exercise, one week at a time. There was only one exercise that I found too hard to do, and that was Exercise 29 where we image ourselves as a corpse decomposing! I have otherwise found every one of them so helpful with so many ways to connect to God.

Each exercise was one that I wanted to practice. I think I identified most with the fantasy exercises, especially Exercise 18, the joyful mysteries of your life. Here we immerse ourselves in joyful times in our lives, remembering details, staying in the moment, experiencing the joy, love. De Mello then recommends that we build an album of these peak experiences to return to in order to help us through difficult times, to keep reminding ourselves of the joy in our life, and the presence of God in those past moments during dry times when God may not feel present.

De Mello writes that when we have memorable experiences we never truly appreciate and take in the joy of the total awareness of what is happening. He asks us to go back again and again to the event to replay it and feel the love we were offered and be nourished again by the experience. He cautions us not to be an observer but put ourselves totally back into the experience. De Mello believes remembering these experiences increases our capacity for joy and consequently opens our life to receive more fully the love of God.

Kelsey: Spiritual Pathways

"There are two quite different ways of leading people on the spiritual pilgrimage, which have often been seen as opposed to each other."

–Morton Kelsey, *Companions on the Inner Way, The Art of Spiritual Guidance.* Paulist Press, 1976.

Kelsey is describing first the sacramental method of spiritual direction where we use spiritual practices such as concrete matter, music, pictures, beads, rituals, symbols to connect to God. The downsize is that these can lead to idolatry, worshipping the means we use to reach God instead of worshipping God. For Episcopalians, it has always been the *Book of Common Prayer* as illustrated by the difficulty when our tradition tries to revise the book. Droves of people leave the church. The same thing may happen in churches when the altar is moved or the order of service or even the prayers are changed. Kelsey calls this method the kataphatic way from the Greek meaning "with images."

Kelsey describes the second path based on the belief that we best connect to God by emptying ourselves of all images, remembering that there is no way to describe or represent the holy. In silence and emptiness, we connect to the God within. The is the apophatic way from the Greek meaning without images. This has been the way of Hinduism, Buddhism, and Christian contemplative forms such as Centering Prayer. Kelsey believes that the downside is that this inner work can occasionally lead to a lack of reaching out to others even though the true result should be connecting the Christ we find within to the Christ in others.

Kelsey encourages us to practice both methods. The two are a necessary part of a well-developed and informed spirituality.

Nouwen: Community

"Community is not a talent show in which we dazzle the world with our combined gifts. Community is the place where our poverty is acknowledged and accepted, not as something we have to learn to cope with as best as we can but as a true source of new life."

–Henri Nouwen, *Bread for the Journey*. Harper San Francisco, 1997.

The Hebrew Bible and the New Testament constantly reveal stories of how God continually calls us to community. This is what enlarges our view of God, keeps our God from being so small as we hear about the God of their understanding from others. In community is where we learn how our gifts our needed and how we don't need to have all the gifts or be in control. In community, we also learn about ourselves as we begin to see that the faults we so dislike in others are often also in ourselves, and in time we see how ugly they are in the ourselves as well and finally pray to be changed.

We also learn about forgiveness as we are forgiven. In community as we attempt to live in harmony we learn about reconciliation, pluralism, connection, a different kind of living than our society often teaches us.

We live in a zero-sum world, where we are taught there is only so much food, so much resources, so many jobs, so much money, so much love to go around. If we give any of what we have away, we will lose it all, we will lose all that we have accumulated, and it will not return, so we store our things in pods and warehouses and even store up love inside of ourselves and don't give it away. We fear if we share, we will lose what we have and not be able to have more.

I learned about the fallacy of zero sum from some of my grandchildren. I once envied their grandparents who lived nearby while we lived far away. I feared there was only so much love my grandchildren could give, and their closer grandparents were going to get most of it. Oh, me. My grandchildren have taught me that they have much more love to give than I can fathom, and how wonderful it can be that they know and share the love of so many living grandparents. This is what we learn in community. We learn about God's love without numbers, love without conditions, love that we cannot hold onto, but love that can only grow if it continually moves and flows in and out of us.

As I meet with spiritual friends I share what I have learned in community and offer living in community as one more way to keep that connection to God which so beautifully lives in others. In return, our community reflects to us the Christ, the God of our understanding which also dwells within ourselves as well.

Charleston: We Are Not Done Yet, Community

"We are not done yet. We may count our progress in inches. We may swim against the deep tides of greed and hate, but we are not done yet. Even if we do not live to see it all, we will be content to be the inspiration, to give all we have to free our world from fear."

–Steven Charleston, Facebook Post.

Bishop Charleston gives us encouragement during difficult times when we are discouraged. This is why God constantly calls us to community. When our lights are dim, we feel we have lost our connection to God, we feel we have not accomplished anything, in fact we believe we are failures, there are others in our community whose lights are on, who are more connected to God, who can encourage and support us until we see a different picture. They are like Simon of Cyrene, briefly carrying our cross. They are like the friends of the paralytic lifting him through the rooftop to Jesus. Then in turn as we heal, it will be our turn to be the encourager.

Often people come for spiritual direction or meet with spiritual friends who indeed have been burned out or feel their life or their ministry is not accomplishing what they had hoped. That is our job as spiritual friends, to show each other where indeed God is working in our lives and how important it is for us to continue to be an inspiration to each other, remembering that we may not see the results. The results may be apparent much later, long after we have lived our lives and our names have been forgotten.

As I grow older, I seem more vividly to remember the people, the teachers, my grandparents, my co-workers and friends who encouraged me, who supported me, who never gave up on me. Most of them are indeed dead, so I can now only thank them by trying to encourage others as they did to me. So today, I share with you Jon Sweeney's new biography of Phyllis Tickle, *Phyllis Tickle, A Life*, where he shares how Phyllis was a major encourager for him and myself as well as so many others.

Butler Bass: Belonging, Community

"Instead of believing, behaving, and belonging, we need to reverse the order to belonging, behaving, and believing. Jesus did not begin with questions of belief. Jesus' public ministry started when he formed a community."

–Diana Butler Bass, *Christianity After Religion: The End of Church and the Birth of a New Spiritual Awakening.* Harper One, 2011.

Diana Butler Bass tries to help us understand what is happening in the present day changing Christian landscape where religion is now no longer the center of a member's life. She reminds us that our religion started with community, not confession. Thomas Watkins from Wilson, North Carolina also tries to explain how our church might change using the South's love of football in an article in *Journal of Preacher* ("Game Day: Becoming a New Church in an Old South," vol. 40, no. 4) "They (fans) are not asked to show their diplomas at the stadium gate."

One of the most frequent questions of those coming for spiritual direction is "I don't know if I believe or what I believe anymore. Maybe I am no longer a Christian." If the person belongs to a confessional denomination or a church of orthodoxy where he or she must believe a certain set of doctrines, this can sometimes be a problem. There are denominations that are churches of orthopraxy where its members are held together because of a way they worship or practice their faith. In that circumstance, a changing belief is considered at times an asset, a sign of growth. Our relationship to God will change as our God becomes larger, as we come to see the Christ in more and more people, people who are very different from ourselves. I often quote that line I first heard from

Alan Jones at a Trinity Wall Street conference at Kanuga in the early 2000's: "the opposite of faith is not doubt, but certainty." Doubting is a sign that God is working in us; our relationship is changing. Sometimes this change in relationship can feel like the movement of the earth's tectonic plates. Sometimes it can be like a volcano erupting. If we can just take it as a good and not a bad thing and try to stay steady, a new relationship, a new life will arise. I remember a quote attributed to Catherine Marshall, "Those who never rebelled against God or at some point in their lives shaken their fists in the face of heaven, have never encountered God at all."

This is also where community is important. In a church that is alive with the spirit, there will be many others who have experienced this awakening who can walk and hold a steady hand when the foundations that we thought were our beliefs are threatened. We come to see that these beliefs are not threatened, but enlarged, and we learn this because of belonging to a community.

Lent 2: Second Week in Lent

De Waal: Living on the Border, Community

"The first step in listening, learning, and changing is to see that different is not dangerous; the second is to be happy and willing to live with uncertainty; the third is to rejoice in ambiguity and to embrace it. It all means giving up the comfort of certainty and realizing that uncertainty can actually be good."

–Esther de Waal, *To Pause at the Threshold, Reflections on Living on the Border.* Morehouse, 2004.

When de Waal wrote this book, she had returned to the home where she had grown up on the border between England and Wales. I met this prolific writer of Benedictine and Celtic spirituality at the College of Preachers at the Washington National Cathedral. She often took up residence there and was accessible during meals to weekly pilgrims like myself seeking respite and learning at this sacred space. This small pocket-sized book is a gem to be read and re-read. De Waal is talking about how we relate to borders and boundaries as she is directly experiencing borders in her day to day living experience. Do we build walls and barriers and fortresses or do we engage in conversation and learn about something different, another culture? She describes the diversity of the world as an icon to let us know that God loves differences. She entices us to be like a porter waiting at the gate of a Benedictine monastery, standing at the "threshold of two worlds," welcoming those who come no matter the time of day, treating each stranger as if it were Christ. This resonates with me as a deacon. Our ministry calls us to go back and forth between two worlds, the church, and the world outside of the church. De Waal also teaches us to honor the threshold or the two worlds and be open to the change, the uncertainty, the contradictions that the different worlds may present to us.

De Waal's concept of thresholds has been helpful in visiting those in hospitals or the homebound. I have learned to pause as I am about the cross the threshold of the door. At hospitals, this is a time to wash my hands at the door. The threshold is a symbolic reminder that I am entering another world. The handwashing is a reminder to leave my agenda at the door. I am there to honor that person and to listen and be present to them. Some of the time I remember.

Wisdom from the Harp, Community

"For the elements changed places with one another,
as on a harp the notes vary the nature of the rhythm,
while each note remains the same."

–Wisdom 19:18

A friend reminds me this was in the scripture in morning prayer today. I read the first part of the Wisdom reading this morning but missed this last part. I hope I won't miss it next time, for this ancient verse so well describes music, but especially the harp. I began a journey with this classical instrument over thirty years ago when my daughter begged for a year to get a harp.

The strings are the white keys of the piano, so if you understand the piano, it is easy. You lean the body against your body so you can not only hear the vibrations but you feel the music within you as well. The harp has taught me so many lessons about life other than the discipline of trying to master a technique for following and plucking the notes.

When one string breaks, it is difficult to continue playing. Part of playing is knowing the relationships of each string to the other. Now there is a gap, large or small which changes the entire road map. I learn I must take the time to replace the string as soon as possible. Then of course it takes, days, weeks for that new string to stretch and be in tune. It must be "mentored" so to speak.

Almost every atmospheric condition changes the harp strings. Constant tuning is mandatory. My husband loves the old joke about harpist. We spend half our time tuning and the other half playing out of tune!

On this musical journey, the harp has become for me an icon for living and working in community. Its constant need for tuning reminds me how much I must try to stay current, learning and staying and in relationship with what is going on in the world around me. If I don't, I become "out of tune" either too sharp or too flat.

I would love to hear from others about life lessons they have learned from a musical instrument.

Listening

"Be a lamp, a lifeboat or a ladder. Help someone's soul heal. Walk out of your house like a shepherd."

–Rumi (1207-1273), "Daily Quotes." InwardOutward.org, May 3, 2018.

Sometimes I think if I were to redesign a program about spiritual direction that 90% of the time would be devoted to listening. My experience is that listening is one of the best tools of the Holy Spirit within us. I am talking about active listen where we clear our heads as much as possible of agendas and what is going on in our lives. We offer up the gift of time for forty-five minutes or an hour to listen to someone else's life. For this short period of time we are given the privilege of caring for the soul of another, helping a person realize God's never-failing presence in his or her own presence.

I sit and all these great ideas come to me as I listen. "I think she would like this book. Changing to this spiritual exercise might be helpful."

I am learning that if I interrupt with my ideas, they often fall on deaf ears, but if I wait until there is silence and speak, the person seems to see and hear better what I might suggest. Sometimes as I wait, I later realize, "no, this was not the right book or spiritual exercise."

I have learned a great deal about listening from my harp. Perhaps you have occasionally noticed a loud buzzing sound when some harpists play. Buzz. One of the reasons for a buzz is that you have plucked a string that is still vibrating from a recent placement of that finger or another finger on that string. You must wait for that string to stop vibrating before you play it again or this annoying sound comes out.

My buzzing harp is reminding me that I must wait for the person I am visiting with to stop talking.

I am learning how to play less buzzing notes and to talk less and listen more at the same time. My buzzing harp string has become my icon for listening.

Listening can become a "lamp, a lifeboat, and a ladder" to the presence of the Holy Spirit in our own lives as well as the lives of our spiritual friends.

Owensby: Changing Our Perspective, Community

"A gestalt shift is a visual switch of perspective. While looking at an unchanging image we see first one thing and then another. For instance, in the picture below you can see a duck. Or a rabbit."

–Jake Owensby, "Looking for God in Messy Places." JakeOwensby.com, March 3, 2018.

In his weekly blog, Looking for God in Messy Places, the fourth bishop of the Episcopal Diocese of Western Louisiana, talks about how we make on interpretation of what we are seeing before we see it. He challenges us to look at some things we think are familiar in another way. His story is about how through Jesus he changed his ideas about God.

Gestalt shifts involve changing our mind about something.

I see Gestalt shifts in spiritual direction as well. Spiritual direction is about caring for the soul. Spiritual friends help us put on a new pair of glasses so we can see God at work in their lives at times when we did not perceive God before. Spiritual friends ask questions like, "how is your heart" instead of "how are you doing." Spiritual friends follow a rule of life where we "bend the knee of the heart" and "listen with the ear of the heart." Spiritual friends help us find our own sacred space inside of each of us as well as finding sacred spaces outside of us in the world. We begin to see what Barbara Brown Taylor describes in her book, *An Altar in the World*.

The Gestalt shift of spiritual friends is that we look beyond the surface and see the Christ in each other, especially in the person we previously were having difficulty with. We begin to see them in a new light, often very wounded just like the rest of us.

–Prayer of Manasseh, p. 91, *Book of Common Prayer.* Church Publishing.
–Prologue to *The Rule of Saint Benedict.*

Parker Palmer: Seeking Sanctuary in Our Own Sacred Spaces

"At times something happens that makes us hypersensitive to all that threatens our souls. Sanctuary is wherever I find safe space to regain my bearings, reclaim my soul, heal my wounds, and return to the world as a wounded healer. It's not merely about finding shelter from the storm: it's about spiritual survival. Today, seeking sanctuary is no more optional for me than church attendance was as a child."

–Parker Palmer, "What We Need to Flourish Is Here." Onbeing.org, September 21, 2016.

Parker Palmer reminds us how important it is to have a safe place, a sanctuary where we can go to and renew our spirit when we are wounded, when all around us is falling apart, when we lose our direction. It is indeed about spiritual survival. I think of people who live in crowded quarters, multiple families in a few rooms, refugees in camps. How do they ever renew their spirit? Perhaps this is factor in their unrest.

I have had so many sanctuaries, my bedroom growing up, a cigar box filled with sacred treasures, my grandparents' home, a school, a dock, a river, a woods, listening to music, playing music, singing, a chapel, a person, many other bedrooms, a church camp, many offices with little altars, a dress shop, books, paintings, a favorite hotel, a writer, a daily walk, museums, phone calls, a chair, a beach, a balcony, a church, special friends.

Today my sanctuary is writing, trying to clear thoughts from my head and move them from my head to my body. I give thanks that somehow these sanctuary places came about at the right time. The seemingly healthiest friends I have all have sanctuaries and are not ashamed or embarrassed to talk about them.

Of course, there are the dangerous sanctuaries, food, alcohol, drugs, work, shopping, relationships which are temporary dwellings built on sand.

Surrender

"The boat I travel in is called Surrender. My two oars are instant forgiveness and gratitude—complete gratitude for the gift of life. I am thankful for the experience of this life, for the opportunity to dance. I get angry, I get mad, but as soon as I remind myself to put my oars in the water, I forgive."

–Balbir Matbur, "Daily Quote." InwardOutward.org, October 19, 2016.

Balbir Matbur as president of Trees for Life for 30 years planted 200 million morning trees in developing countries. I thank the daily words from Inward Outward from the Church of the Saviour in Washington for introducing him to me. Matbur's exceptional life is a story of constant surrender: immigrating to Wichita from India with no family contacts, mowing lawns, becoming world known in business, developing a mysterious illness, leaving his business career, and starting an international nonprofit to plant trees in developing countries. The morning trees survive in dry conditions, its leaves are nutritious in vitamins A and C and calcium, and its seeds are used to purify water.

Matbur's words are indeed words of peace that I hear in so many disciplines across all religious barriers. When I can forgive, when I am filled with gratitude, I stay out of trouble and find peace. What an image. We are in a boat called surrender and our two oars are gratitude and forgiveness that keep that boat moving on course. I can imagine rowing on a river, not too big of a river and not too big of a boat. I will need some other passengers with me who can take over the oars when I become too tired, who will read to me and let me rest or just allow me to soak in the scenery.

Mary Dwyer: Forgiveness

"Forgiveness is not forgetting, not condoning not a form of absolution, not a pretense, not a once and for all decision, and not a sign of weakness but of strength."

–Mary Dwyer, "Learning to Forgive." One Day Retreat of Contemplative Outreach, St. Mark's, February 10, 2018.

Last weekend at a Forgiveness Workshop with Mary Dwyer from Contemplative Outreach, Ltd., at St. Mark's we learn some basics to start the journey of forgiveness. She reminds us that forgiveness is the only conditional part of the Lord's Prayer, "forgive our sins, as we forgive others."

Reconciliation involves both parties. Forgiveness involves only one party.

Mary cautioned us about forgiving too soon.

She used the process from Fr. William A. Meninger's book, *The Process of Forgiveness.* The first stage of beginning to forgive involves claiming the hurt, often by writing about it. Telling our story also is a big part in Bishop Tutu's book, *The Book of Forgiving.* In the second stage toward healing we feel guilt that maybe we did something wrong for this to happen. Here we are healed by comforting our inner child. In the third stage we see ourselves as the victim. Mary gave examples of how so many people get stuck in this stage. Their whole life is centered around some hurt many years ago. Support groups help in this stage as we see we are not the only ones who have been harmed. In the fourth stage we become very anger about the hurt. Anger brings with it a huge amount of energy and clarity.

If we can transform that energy, we can then start healing as we release this energy and become whole again. What helps me the most is the knowledge that the person who has harmed me is still hurting me as long I cannot forgive them.

Mary then described a process of active imagination with God and the person who has harmed us called the Forgiveness Prayer. After a period of Centering Prayer, we imagine our own sacred space with God very close to us. She imagines she is sitting in God's lap. My sacred space would be sitting on the white sandy beach by the ocean watching the waves come gently in as the sea gulls fly in and out at the water's edge. We then invite someone who has harmed us to come into our space. We tell them all that they have done to harm us. Then we ask them if we have harmed them and then ask them for forgiveness. Sometimes having a picture of the person who harmed us may be helpful as we speak to him or her. This is not a one-time event but may require many encounters. For me, the Forgiveness Prayer is so helpful when the person who harmed me refuses to talk about it. The Prayer allows us to talk to that person in a safe place where we cannot be harmed again, but also to acknowledge mistakes we made as well.

Mary also recommends praying daily for the person who has harmed us until we are ready to forgive.

Lent 3: Third Week of Lent

Kidd, Brueggmann: Forgiveness

"People, in general, would rather die than forgive. It's that hard."

–Sue Monk Kidd, *The Secret Life of Bees.* Penguin, 2003.

For myself, if someone has harmed me, I begin to think about them all the time and what I would like to do to them, expose them. They live rent free in my head and in essence become my higher power, my God. I do not want this person to be my God, my higher power. That is what brings me back to start the work of forgiveness. Yes, for me it is extremely hard work. Forgiveness is not forgetting. There are things we should never forget: the Holocaust, the Armenian genocide, slavery, abuse, 9/ 11, Hurricanes Camille, Frederic, Ivan, Katrina, and now Harvey and Irma.

Walter Brueggmann writes about forgiveness especially from what we learn in the Old Testament. He writes that forgiveness is made impossible in a system of deeds-consequence when deeds have an unbreakable tight predictable connection to consequences with no way out. This is the law, and if you break it, this is what will happen to you. Amen. This is the basis of much religious preaching of "hell, fire, and damnation," trying to frighten people into a moral life. Brueggmann believes that forgiveness is only possible when we realize the astonishing readiness of God to reach beyond deeds-consequences, to offer continually to us unlimited restoration and extravagant forgiveness. There is nothing, nothing that we can do for which God does not forgive us, and we are called to do the same. When we begin to lead a life of pardoning and newness, we start to see the world not through our grievances but through gratitude. It is a new life, a different life. We saw it in Nelson Mandela who forgives his guards of his 27 years of imprisonment as he walks out of prison. He tells others who are harboring resentments and grievances, "if I do not forgive them, I am still in prison." Buddhists call it the Great Compassion.

–Walter Brueggemann, "The Impossible Possibility of Forgiveness." *Journal of Preachers,* Pentecost, 2015.

Sue Monk Kidd: False Selves

"Your joy is your sorrow unmasked."

–Kahlil Gibran

I especially relate to Sue Monk Kidd's naming of our false selves or masks we wear that we initially put on to protect ourselves from the difficulties we encounter from our very beginnings, but these identities are not our true self. These are similar but an expanded, feminine form of Fritz Kunkel's four: Turtle, Star, Eternal Boy, and Tyrant. Kidd describes the Little Girl with a Curl (pleaser, very good), Tinsel Star (overachiever, perfectionist, performer), Rapunzel (waiting to be rescued), Little Red Hen (duty), Chicken Little (fear-based like Turtle), Tin Woodman (no heart or connection to body). She offers some advice as how to recognize these false selves and how to take off the mask with each of them.

In *When the Heart Waits*, Kidd challenges us to think about who we would be if all of the roles we play were suddenly stripped away. I connect to her writing about the difficulty of letting go or diapause. I remember my difficulty completely retiring from medicine. I worked four days a week, then twice a week, then twice a month, and finally one day a month. It is so hard to let go of a persona that has been ours for forty years.

Kidd describes the tension that arises when we recognize these false selves that have dominated our lives. She describes an orphanage of banished selves still crying out inside of us. What happens when we still hear the "ego logic" of the Star and the Red Hen driving us to promote ourselves or responding to the Little Girl with the Curl who feels abandoned and unloved and wants to please? What happens when the

Star decides not to perform because she learns more about God's love and no longer needs to be approved by others? I remember this was my persona from an early age when my grandfather first put me up on a picnic table when I as maybe 9 or 10 years old to play my accordion at our family 4th of July picnic. She has been so much a part of my life for so long.

On the other hand, we know we are connected to our real or true self when we respond out of love rather than fear, and honesty rather than approval seeking. The Tin Man is healed by reconnecting our body to our mind, heart and soul by creative dialoguing with our body. I am reminded of the body exercises of Anthony DeMello.

Kidd believes that when we do find our true self and Rapunzel no longer gets someone to rescue her, and the Woodman recovers his heart and embraces his feelings and body, and the Little Girl with the Curl finds her own voice, and the Red Hen stops taking care of everyone else, and the Pleaser stops pleasing, that other people we live with may have difficulty. They no longer know how to react to us as our true self.

Kidd calls us to hold our false selves in our hands and trace our fingers over the masks we wear and begin to find the real person God created us to be.

Charleston: Wisdom

"I think spiritual wisdom is not the measure of how much we know, but how much we have learned. Knowledge can become static, a museum of dogmas, a warehouse of opinions. We discover wisdom over and over again when what we think we know meets what we have never encountered before."

–Bishop Steven Charleston, Facebook Post.

There is a chasm between intellect and wisdom. My husband, Robert, a prolific reader of history, shared with me a story by the journalist, David Halberstam. Halberstam, the author of the 1972 book, *The Best and the Brightest*, about the origins of the Vietnam War, detailed in his book Lyndon's Johnson first visits to JFK's cabinet meetings with among others, the brilliant McNamara and Kennedy's advisor, Ted Sorensen. Others assembled were also the brightest minds in the country. Johnson went back to his old friend, Sam Rayburn, the longest running Speaker of the House in our country, just overcome with a feeling of awe and perhaps inadequacy. Rayburn reminded Johnson that there is a difference between wisdom and knowledge or intellect. Rayburn is quoted as saying, "They may be just as intelligent as you say. But I'd feel a helluva lot better if just one of them had ever run for sheriff."

Knowledge or intellect is learning, investigating, researching, and studying facts and data. Wisdom is knowledge with experience, discerning which facts are true, how the knowledge can best be applied to your life.

Knowledge is knowing where babies come from. Wisdom is knowing how to care for them. Knowledge is doing the distance between here and New York City. Wisdom is knowing what to pack for the trip.

We belong to the information age. There is no lack of information and data. All of us on this spiritual journey are gathering information about a multitude of spiritual tools, spiritual knowledge, to use to guide and help ourselves and others.

Wisdom will be digesting what we learn, taking it inside, and seeing what is truly the right meal for us as well as for those who come for spiritual direction at different times in our lives and theirs. A major tool in discerning wisdom is listening with the heart to the spiritual friends who visit with us and listening actively to hear how our experience and the present world and nature around us intersects with our lives and theirs.

Wythe: Spirituality at the Workplace

"The first step to preserving the soul in our individual lives is to admit that the world has a soul also and is somehow participating with us in our work and destiny. That there is a sacred otherness to the world that is breathtakingly helpful simply because it is not us."

–David Whyte, *The Heart Aroused: Poetry and the Preservation of the Soul in Corporate America*. Doubleday Business, 1994.

In his book *The Heart Aroused*, poet David Wythe writes about taking our spirituality with us to the workplace where it is so desperately needed by ourselves and others. He believes that preservation of the soul means giving up our desire in the scheduled workplace not to have the unscheduled meeting. My experience as well is that God drops into my life into the interruptions not on my agenda.

Whyte believes we must relinquish a belief that the world owes us a place on a divinely ordained career ladder. We have a place in the world but it is constantly shape-shifting. Our deeper struggles can be our greatest spiritual and creative assets and the doors to creativity. The Greeks said that if the gods really wanted to punish someone, they granted that person everything they wished for. The soul's ability to experience joy in the workplace is commensurate with our ability to feel grief. We walk into corporate offices looking like full-grown adults but many parts of us are still playing emotional catch-up from the grief and traumas of childhood which unconsciously refuse to grow any older until the trauma is resolved.

The most dangerous time for a male is around nine o'clock on Monday morning and then the few months following his retirement when more injuries and illnesses occur. One is a death caused by carrying the burden and the other the ability to live without the burden. Work almost always becomes a platform for self-righteous moralizing. Hurrying from one workstation to another, we hope the hurrying itself can grant us importance we seek. Wythe suggests that slowing for a moment, we might open up to the emptiness at the center.

Wythe reminds us how astonishing it is to see how we shrink from the things that nourish our soul and take on every possible experience to quit it. I personally did this for dream work as I became too busy in my "church work" to go to my longtime dream group. I also see this continually in spiritual direction where I have a hard time fitting my own spiritual director into my own "busy schedule."

Morning Wake Up

"I will take you from among all nations; *
and gather you from all lands to bring you home.
I will sprinkle clean water upon you; *
and purify you from false gods and uncleanness.
A new heart I will give you *
and a new spirit put within you.
I will take the stone heart from your chest *
and give you a heart of flesh.
I will help you walk in my laws *
and cherish my commandments and do them.
You shall be my people, *
and I will be your God."

–Ezekiel 36:24-28

"A Song of Ezekiel," *Enriching our Worship I, Supplemental Liturgical Materials* prepared by The Standing Liturgical Commission, Church Publishing Incorporated, New York, 1997.

When people ask how to start their day, this is one suggestion that keeps coming to mind, especially if the person starts her day with a daily bath or shower. A priest I knew in my diaconal training shared that he sings this canticle each morning in his shower. This is an image that has stayed with me for many years. I am not good at memorizing scripture, but for those who are, I cannot think of a better way to start the day. Even if I cannot memorize the scripture, perhaps I can remember some of the lines. I am asking God to sprinkle clean water on me, to purify me from false gods. My favorite false gods are fame, recognition, and work, busyness. I am asking God for a new heart, a new way to love, especially to love those who seem unlovable, different, those who seem to punch all my egocentric buttons that become harder and harder to hide, and those

I perceive have harmed me. I pray for a new spirit, the Holy Spirit, God's will, not my own will, to live inside of me and to lead me. I am well acquainted with and do not like the stone heart that quietly and subtly sneaks into me and judges others and myself. Take that hard stone heart out of my chest. It is a too heavy and painful burden to carry. I pray for a heart that accepts my humanness and the humanness of others. I will try to follow the guidelines I think God has given me. Help me not to believe in my hubris that I am better than others and above the laws you have asked us to follow. I want to stay connected today to you, God, even if it is a thin thread. Perhaps I can remember clean water, no false gods today, a new heart, a new spirit, no stone heart, no hubris, staying connected for just one more day.

First Soul Friend

"So there is a movement from the soul to God, from God to the soul, and from the soul to society and the world."

–Kenneth Leech, *Soul Friend: An Invitation to Spiritual Direction.* HarperOne, 1992.

Kenneth Leech's book *Soul Friend: An Invitation to Spiritual Direction* was the first book I read on spiritual direction over thirty years ago. Something was calling me to be more connected with other spiritual friends. I was going to a counselor who was helping me deal with life on life's terms, but somehow, I instinctively knew I needed a friend whom I knew was caring for my soul, concentrating on helping me see the God of my understanding working in my life. I had learned in my medical practice the importance of sharing ideas and consulting with others. I learned from many mistakes that when I tried to make decisions without getting input from others, I so often went down the wrong path, made the wrong diagnosis.

How do you find someone you can trust with your soul? Spiritual directors were rare breeds at that time. It had to be someone I trusted with my fears and secrets. I knew I shared my life with my family members, but my direction or path to God always affected them directly or indirectly. I knew I needed to talk or be with someone who was not explicitly affected by the insights we might have. After some time, I did find another friend in a book group. She as well was seeking a soul mate, a spiritual friend. We read together Leech's book. I know Leech had so much to teach us, but this is the message we decided to concentrate on.

We met once a week. We each told what was going on in our life, our secret worries, our concerns, our fears, where we thought God might be working in our life. We each talked without interruption or interpretation. There was no advice to the other or empathy or sympathy. We just listened. Then we prayed for each other, specifically for each other's concerns. I am sure Leech would have wanted us to do more, but that was a start for both of us. In essence we were connected to God by telling our secrets to someone else. In doing so these secrets lost their power over us and somehow, we entered the secret place inside of us where God was dwelling. It was a start. I learned a little about how the power of secrets and fears can seal us off from God. We no longer meet but we are still friends and still trust each other and give thanks for this time when our journeys brought us together and started both of us on a new journey. This kind of a friend is invaluable, a gift from God. If you are looking for one, keep it in your prayers, and let us know your experience with a treasured spiritual friend.

Barbara Brown Taylor: Spiritual Practices, Movies, Short Stories

"Anything can become a spiritual practice once you are willing to approach it that way—once you let it bring you to your knees and show you what is real, including who you really are, who other people are, and how near God can be when you have lost your way."

–Barbara Brown Taylor, *An Altar in the World*. Harper One, 2010.

I have been in groups that watched for the presence of God in movies, not necessarily religious movies. One of my favorites is *Places in the Heart* where Sally Fields as a recently widowed farmer's wife in rural Texas during the depression takes in a blind boarder, John Malkovich, and with the help of an African American drifter, Danny Glover, raises and picks cotton to keep her farm. Stop here if you do not want to know more, but the movie ends with all of the characters living and dead, black and white, murdered victim and murderer, kind and unkind, faithful and unfaithful passing communion and love to each other at their local rural church.

I am in another group that reads contemporary short stories to find the voice of God. We have used a four-volume series, *Listening for God* edited by an English professor from Yale University, Paula Carlson, and a professor of Religion, Peter Hawkins. One of my favorite stories is "A Small Good Thing" by Raymond Carver about a couple whose child dies and the baker who had made him a birthday cake. Spoiler alert! This story also ends with the three of them having a form of communion late at night at the baker's shop.

We find communion, spiritual practices all around us in our daily life if we have eyes to see, hears to ear, when we can live in the present and reach out and see what is going on with our neighbor right in front of us.

Lent 4: Fourth Week of Lent

Slow Down…Waiting

"When I am told that waiting seems to belong to the heart of the spiritual life, I'm not pleased, for I want answers, direction, clarity—and I want them pronto…"

–Robert Barron, "What Are You Waiting For?" *U.S. Catholic.* December 2003.

In this article, Barron starts out with that old joke about the pilot who announces that he has good news and bad news. The bad news is that they are totally lost. The good news is that they are making excellent time!

My experience is that spiritual friends initially come to talk because they are consciously or unconsciously in some kind of pain, and like the rest of us seek relief, answers, hopefully very soon. This is something to talk about early on about being aware that staying connected to God requires much waiting. "Those who wait upon the Lord will renew their strength; they will mount up with wings as eagles; they shall run, and not be weary, and they shall walk, and not faint" (Isaiah 40:31-1). This is a good verse that most people may know and can help all of us to remember when we find ourselves impatient. We will experience times when we will fly and walk and not be tired, but waiting is still a major part of the relationship. 12-step groups talk about not leaving before the miracle happens.

I have learned a few exercises from my life as a physician about waiting. I would often go to meetings or have patients or other doctors that would keep me waiting. I had those huge ego experiences of "I am very important. You should not keep me waiting. Don't you know how valuable my time is?" When overcome with these thoughts, I end up mad, arrogant, testy when the person or group finally come. This is never helpful for the interaction. Gradually I learn, that when I find myself waiting, that this is an opportunity to pray for that person or group before we meet, or it is an opportunity to meditate, calm my soul before the meeting. Waiting becomes a gift from that person which makes all the difference in my relationship with those I am meeting with as well as my relationship with God. The same is true about waiting for God. Goodness knows, God spends a great deal of time waiting for us.

Of course, centering prayer, meditation, contemplation, lectio divina are also more exercises about waiting.

Spiritual writer, Michael Vinson, suggests a waiting exercise of remembering times in our lives when by some miracle we do wait and the miracle happens. Perhaps we wait talking to someone about a situation before we hear the whole story. Another spiritual writer, Jane Wolfe, responds to Michael in his blog that God will always give us a nudge when it is time to respond and act after we spend time waiting. Jane reminds us of Mary giving Jesus that nudge at the wedding at Cana when it was now time for him to do something!

–"Sit and Wait." Friday Food, jmichaelvinson.com, February 24, 2017.

MLK: Next Right Thing

"Faith is taking the first step even when you don't see the whole staircase."

–Martin Luther King, Jr.

This past week my husband and I have been remembering 50th anniversary of the death of Martin Luther King, Jr in Memphis, April 4, 2018, and the events leading up to it and afterwards. We were both senior medical students in Memphis during those troubled times when the world seemed to be falling apart. King left us so many legacies.

Today I am thinking most about how he started out in the civil rights movement becoming a leader in the Montgomery, Alabama, bus boycott which began in December1955 after Rosa Parks was arrested for sitting in the front of a bus and lasted for 385 days. King was 26, the new pastor of Dexter Avenue Baptist Church in Montgomery, the capital of Alabama. He supposedly was selected by the African American community to lead the bus boycott because he was new and had not been intimidated by the white community nor had he aligned himself with the various factions in the black community. During the boycott, King was arrested and his home was bombed. King's articulate and nonviolent leadership brought him into national prominence.

King also wrote in his book, *Stride Toward Freedom*, about a spiritual experience as he sat one midnight at his kitchen table after another bomb threat. As he was ready to give up, he felt a divine inner presence that took away his fears and uncertainly, ready to face whatever came that sustained him for the rest of his life. I think this is one of the experiences he is speaking about when he refers to "going to the mountain and hearing the truth."

King did not decide to go to Montgomery to lead a bus boycott or become the leader of the civil rights movement. He most probably went to be a good minister like his father and have a family, but a situation arose, he was chosen, and he stepped in. Certainly, his family background of three generations of ministers and all his training as a minister allowed him to be that leader, but that had not been his goal.

I see this as a message to all of us that we may be trained to be one thing, but we may be called to do something else that we never realized that we had been trained to do all along. Each of us, like Martin, will be called at some time to speak our truth. We most probably will not think we are prepared. We may be given a job because we are young or old and inexperienced, or no one else wants the job. Every biblical story of leadership speaks to this kind of call.

Tonight, I am thinking of the young high school students who are today leading a fight for gun control after an attack at their school.

My experience is that this is one of the ways God works, and the lives of King, Moses, Abraham, the disciples, David, Mary, Joseph, Paul, Esther, St. Benedict, St. Francis, St. Ignatius, Bill Wilson, Dr. Bob, and these students from Marjory Stoneman Douglas High School in Florida exemplify it.

Phyllis Tickle: Divine Hours

"Prayer is a nonlocative, nongeographic space that one enters at one's one peril, for it houses God during those few moments of one's presence there, and what is there will most surely change everything that comes into it."

Phyllis Tickle, *Phyllis Tickle: Essential Spiritual Writings*. Church Publishing, 2018.

Phyllis Tickle was a prolific writer, amazing lecturer, rarely speaking from notes, and founding religion editor for *Publishers Weekly* as well as a great mentor and friend. My thank you to her would be to attempt to continue the kindness and encouragement she showed to me. She may be remembered for her analysis of *The Emergent Christian Church*, but I most treasure her *Divine Hours*, a series of books of observance of the fixed-hour of prayer for spring, summer, fall, and winter. I know she not only wrote about it, she practiced it. I remember seeing her slipping away at meetings for a few minutes to pray at one of the fixed hours of morning, midday, vespers, or compline. Phyllis' books allow us to follow a fixed time of prayer no matter where we are in time or place. She brought back an ancient rule of life to modern times and reminded us how this would change our lives, teaching that we would never be the same after experiencing the practice. I am not as faithful as Phyllis, but instead practice the fixed hours of prayer at certain seasons of the year, sometimes for only a week or a month, sometimes for a whole season. She also wrote an entire book of fixed prayers for night offices for those who have difficulty sleeping or who work at night, prayers at midnight, night watch, and dawn. Phyllis has written prayer books for *Christmastide*, *Eastertide*, as well as a convenient pocket edition of *The Fixed Hours*. There can be no more trusted or beloved friend to keep close by or carry with you during the day or night or during the earth seasons of the year than Phyllis Tickle.

Merton: Prayer as Distraction

"If my prayer is centered in myself, if it seeks only an enrichment of my own self, my prayer itself will be my greatest potential distraction. Full of my own curiosity, I have eaten of the tree of Knowledge and torn myself away from myself and from God. I am left rich and alone and nothing can assuage my hunger: everything I touch turns into a distraction."

–Thomas Merton, *Thoughts in Solitude*. Farrar, Straus and Giroux, 1999.

What a great gift from Merton to remind us of what may be the problem if our prayer life is no longer meaningful and rich, if we seem to lose the connection. Our first question should be, "Is my prayer life centered around myself?" Unfortunately, it is rare that we can really see that in ourselves. It often takes talking to someone else about their stale prayers and seeing that loneliness and isolation and self-center in them. Then the "ah ha" moment comes internally, "The same is also true for me!" We constantly learn from each other consciously or unconsciously.

We also so often realize our egocentricity in community as we see it and abhor it in others and then by Grace realize it is also in ourselves. The change for ourselves, however, so often comes as we withdraw from community in silence, contemplation, and meditation, centering prayer, so many ways for change, to again be aware of that connection to God that was always there. Instead of trying to change the other, we see the gold in the difficulty and see the call to change ourselves which paradoxically calls us to place our center on love of God and others instead of only loving ourselves.

Crafton: Praying for Others

"I can compare prayer to a river-strong, clean, swift, carrying everything along in its powerful current. When I pray, I have stepped into the river and allowed it to carry me. When I pray for you, I have taken your hand and together we step into the river and let it carry us with power."

–Barbara Crafton, *The AlsoLife*. Morehouse, 2016.

Episcopal priest and well-known speaker and writer, Barbara Crafton, teaches us a different view of prayer. It is surrender prayer, prayer of few words, feeling the power of prayer as we pray, bringing others with us into prayer. It is prayer that comes with sitting, swimming, or walking in silence and simply waiting for the Spirit's lead.

Swimming is still a favorite exercise. I can indeed visualize those in my prayers swimming or walking in the water with me. This is an even more powerful image swimming in a river or the ocean where we surrender to let the current move us.

Crafton also writes about prayer as connecting ourselves, aligning ourselves with the energy of the love of God. Prayer is loving, loving God, loving ourselves, loving our neighbor. Some people image Jesus in prayer and walk with or carry friends to Jesus and leave the person they are praying for in Jesus' arm. I so often have used this prayer image when praying for my children and now grandchildren.

For some kneeling at the rail for Eucharist is an image used in prayer. We can image walking with or bringing friends in need with us in prayer to that rail and kneeling with and beside them. This image also helps me in praying for enemies or those with whom I am having difficulty. It is hard to keep hate in my heart when my enemy is kneeling beside me waiting as I am for the body and blood of Christ.

Benedictine Life

"Listen my child with the ear of your heart."

–Prologue of *The Rule of Saint Benedict.*

I keep returning to the Rule of Benedict. "Listen with the ear of your heart" is in the first line of the prologue to *The Rule of Saint Benedict*, a pattern of living in community written by St. Benedict of Nursia in the sixth century during the dark ages and is still used by Benedictines fifteen centuries later. The rule is a balanced model of life that is a radical alternative to a culture out of control. It was written for monastic life, but it has been translated to a way of life for any seeking a pattern of spiritual discipline for living a rule of life in the world. The day is organized around regular periods of private and communal prayer, sleep, work, recreation, hospitality, and study.

Joan Chitister's book, *The Rule of Benedict: A Spirituality for the 21st Century* is used by the Community of Hope International, a program equipping and supporting lay pastoral caregivers to be ministers to all conditions of people needing pastoral care. The Community of Hope International emphasizes developing skills and spiritual practices immersing ministers in Benedictine spirituality in community. Chitister's book can be used privately or in group discussions of the rule. She writes a very helpful meditation and interpretation after each selected part of the rule that can be read in daily segments.

A busy Memphis lawyer, John McQuiston has written another concise modern interpretation of the Rule of Benedict called *Always We Begin Again* that is pocket sized so it is easily carried with you during the day.

A third book is *Spirituality for Everyday Living: An Adaptation of the Rule of St. Benedict* by Brian Taylor. This is another offering to help those not living in a monastery to experience Benedict's rule of obedience and stability in relationships with others. This is living in the balanced tension of the paradox of turning our lives over to a higher power but trying to stay in relationship with others and not staying stagnant but being able to change and grow.

Esther de Waal names it in the title of her book of reflections or meditations in *Benedict's Rule: Living with Contradiction*. Esther de Waal also gives us in *To Pause at the Threshold* numerous Benedictine and Celtic reflections and prayers for us to practice when we cross a threshold of a door going from one room to another. She invites us to say a short prayer, trying to leave the "baggage" in our heads behind and being open to a new experience. This can be helpful when visiting the sick or homebound, as we enter their hospital room or front door.

There are so many other books on Benedictine spirituality, but these are five that have made a difference in my life and the ones I give to people seeking a more patterned or spiritual rule of life. Again, I would love to hear from you about the books on Benedictine spirituality that have made a difference in your life.

Growing in Benedictine Spirituality

"Together (the three vows) are not, as they might seem at first glance about negation, restriction, and limitation...They involve us in the need to face a number of very basic demands: the need not to run away, the need to be open to change, the need to listen... And yet the paradox is that they bring freedom, true freedom."

–Esther de Waal, *Seeking God: The Way of St. Benedict.* The Liturgical Press, 1984.

This weekend I had the privilege of reviewing the Rule of Benedict with an amazing group from St. Nikolas and St. Peter's Episcopal Churches learning how to be pastoral caregivers through a program called Community of Hope. Following a Rule of Benedictine spirituality involves taking a vow to seek spiritual growth by connecting to three areas of support in our lives: conversion, obedience and stability. Stability speaks to our connecting to a certain community, at work, at a place of worship, within a family, in a recovery group, in the world. Obedience speaks to seeking to look for the Christ in all we meet, especially in that community. Conversion or change occurs as we seek Christ in others in our community and they in turn now see and reflect Christ in us. That Christ within us then leads us to growth.

A former priest I worked with, Peggy Bosmyer, compared this concept to a sailing ship. We get into the boat. We make a commitment to be in the boat. That is stability. How we direct our boat is the rudder, that is obedience, being obedient to attempting to see Christ in others. The Holy Spirit, the wind. then moves the sails bringing about conversion, a change in movement as we now see and feel Christ in ourselves. Seeing

Christ in our neighbor leads and reflects back to us the Christ within us. That Christ within us then leads us to change to a new life.

Lent 5: Fifth Week of Lent

De Mello: Ignatian Exercises and More

"This is the spirit in which we embark upon Ignatian contemplations. Through the simple childlike use of our fantasy we attain a truth far beyond fantasy, the truth of mystery, the truth of the mystics."

–Anthony de Mello, *Sadhana: A Way to God.* Image Books, 1978.

De Mello offers many awareness exercises to know and feel the presence of Christ especially in prayer. In one exercise, we imagine that Jesus is sitting in an empty chair beside us. He reminds us that we can start our prayer in our head, but our prayers will become stale and dry if we do not move to our senses and the heart, out of a place of thinking and talking and moving into a place of feeling, sensing loving, and being intuitive.

De Mello uses Ignatian contemplation to help us become a part of a scene from the life of Christ to enhance our reading of scripture and our prayer life. He reminds us of others who experience God using Ignatian contemplation. Francis of Assisi took Jesus down from the Cross and knew he was no longer dead. Teresa of Avila felt closest when she was present with Christ as he agonized in the garden. Ignatius of Loyola became a servant accompanying Mary and Joseph to Bethlehem.

Scripture: Ignatian Exercises

"Take a passage from scripture that you enjoy. Ignatius invites you to enter into the scene by 'composing the place' by imagining yourself in the story with as much detail as you can muster."

–James Martin, *The Jesuit Guide to Almost Everything*. HarperOne 2010.

Ignatius practiced spirituality by taking his students and himself deep into the story of scripture in their imagination and sometimes literally. We start with the senses, seeing, hearing, smelling, tasting, feeling. As we live inside the story, Ignatius asks us to pay attention to what insights might come. Soon in our imaginary journey, we can travel in time and find ourselves back in the scripture with a different understanding than when we are just intellectualizing the story in our head.

At the front of the refectory at the College of Preachers at the National Cathedral, in stain glassed was written, "if you do not dramatize the message, they will not listen." You can see this from many angles, but what it came to mean to me was that my job as preacher was to help those in the congregation "experience" the scripture, usually the gospel, as Ignatius is asking us to do. My experience was I could best do this by taking myself and all who would like to make a journey into the story, be one of the characters, feel his feelings, know his hopes and fears, his frustrations, his loves, his passions, his humanness. The same is true for advice to spiritual friends whose study of scripture has become stale. It is hard to become dry when we actually go into a story in scripture and become a part of it. We will hear voices we have never heard before.

I was first exposed to this Ignatian exercises and this method of studying scripture in a small purple book, *The Spiritual Exercises of St. Ignatius* in the Image Classics. I know there are now so many more. A priest I work with, Michael McCain, recommended this one by James Martin as well.

Thomas Keating, Cynthia Bourgeault: Centering Prayer

"God can be held fast and loved by means of love, but by thought never."

–Ira Progoff, *The Cloud of Unknowing*. Delta Books, 1957.

In Centering Prayer, we select a sacred word as the symbol of our willingness to surrender to the presence of God.

We sit comfortably with closed eyes in silence and then introduce the sacred word.

Whenever thoughts return, we silently speak the sacred word.

At the end of the prayer period, we remain silent with eyes closed for a few minutes.

Thomas Keating suggests practicing Centering Prayer for twenty minutes twice a day.

Is Centering Prayer a simply letting go of one thought after another? That can certainly be our subjective experience of the practice, and this is exactly the frustration we sometimes encounter during Centering Prayer and Lectio Divina.

Keating tells the story of a nun who tries out her first twenty-minute experience of Centering Prayer and then laments, "Father Thomas, I'm such a failure at this prayer. In twenty minutes, I've had ten thousand thoughts!"

"How lovely," responds Keating. "Ten thousand opportunities to return to God."

Keating emphasizes that Centering Prayer is indeed a pathway of return to God, and this may be what the writer of Cloud of the Unknowing was trying to tell us.

We also need to remember that the benefit of Centering Prayer is usually not during the prayer time, but later in the day or week when we feel God's presence where or when we need it or never knew it before. It is expressed best in several of the promises in the *Big Book of Alcoholics Anonymous*, "We will intuitively know how to handle situations which used to baffle us."

–Adapted from Cynthia Bourgeault, *The Heart of Centering Prayer: Nondual Christianity in Theory and Practice*. Shambhala, from Richard Rohr's Daily Meditation, February 11, 2017 with Cynthia Bourgeault as guest writer.

–*Big Book of Alcoholic Anonymous*. Alcoholic Anonymous World Services Inc. 4th edition, 2001.

Keating: Centering Prayer 2

"Silence is God's first language; everything else is a poor translation."

–Thomas Keating, *Invitation to Love: The Way of Christian Contemplation*. Bloomsbury Academic, 1994.

I daily talk with spiritual friends who are prisoners to the business of their minds trying to keep pace with the business of the world. It is natural to see Centering Prayer as an escape from the world, but Keating and Cynthia Bourgeault remind us that this spiritual practice is instead a reconnecting to God. This is not a one-time practice like a shot of penicillin for an infection of pneumonia. It is more like a daily heart medication which can strengthen a muscle that perhaps has not been cared for in the past.

Another difficult concept is that the change that takes place in a person's live is usually most felt some time later than when he or she sits and practice the exercise. The change also may be more prominent in others than in the one practicing centering prayer. God is the healer.

We put ourselves in position to be healed in centering prayer.

I also have friends who as with most other exercises find this one easier to stay with it when they meet on a regular basis with others doing Centering Prayer.

Thomas Keating, "The Method of Centering Prayer: The Prayer of Consent," Contemplative Outreach, www.contemplativeoutreach.org

Centering Prayer: A New Heart

"A new heart I will give you, and a new spirit I will put within you;
and I will remove from your body the heart of stone
and give you a heart of flesh."

–Ezekiel 36:26

Thomas Keating and those who practice centering prayer, a contemporary form of contemplative prayer, believe that the daily 20 minutes of silence is not just prayer with God but also divine therapy, where during that time of quiet, God, the Holy Spirit, slips in and heals us of old and new wounds. They believe that silence may be the language of God where God can perform "open heart" surgery during this time of silent prayer, transforming us into our true self, unloading our over-identification with the "false self" which developed since birth in order for us to survive in an imperfect world. Keating has written extensively about centering prayer. Best known among his works is a trilogy, *Open Mind, Open Heart*, which is considered the handbook for his method of centering prayer, Invitation to Love, about the stages of spiritual growth, and third, Intimacy with God, which describes more deeply what goes on psychologically during centering prayer and Lectio Divina and addresses the theological basis for centering prayer. Other books to use to study about Centering Prayer are Thomas Keating's *Open Mind, Open Heart*; *Invitation to Love*; and *Intimacy with God: An Introduction to Centering Prayer*.

Jesus Prayer

"Lord God, Lamb of God, that takest away the sins of the world, have mercy on me. "

This is a modification of the Agnus Dei recited or sung in the Eucharist or communion service at what is called the fraction as the celebrant breaks the consecrated bread. The prayer is also a modification of the ancient Jesus Prayer, "Lord Jesus Christ, Son of God, have mercy on me." I have used this modification for years, on awakening, during the day, especially during difficult times, and as I fall asleep. When the Jesus Prayer or a modification is repeated continually, it is considered a Prayer of the Heart, opening the heart, with unceasing prayer as called for by Paul in two of his letters: Romans 12:12 and 1 Thessalonians 5:17.

I have only been to one General Convention of the Episcopal Church. What I most remember is attending a special lecture by Henri Nouwen. I continually give thanks that I took time out of a busy day to go. I do not remember a word Nouwen said, but I do remember his presence. It was loving, accepting, not centered on himself, at peace with himself, the closest thing I have seen to a holy presence. I can still feel that presence in his writings. Nouwen's theme of praying the prayer of the heart in *Reaching Out: The Three Movements of the Spiritual Life* moves our prayers from the head to the heart, realizing that the answers to questions and the presence of God are in our heart. Nouwen's thoughts remind me of the spiritual exercises of DeMello who uses imaging our body and breath to move from our head to our heart and body. One of Nouwen's major recommendations to make this movement from head to heart is using the Jesus Prayer.

The Jesus Prayer has been a part of my being, most particularly when I find myself living in fear, but I have never said it unceasing 3000 times a day, then 6000, then 12,000 times a day as was recommended by the 5th century Egyptian desert fathers and by the 19th century Russian monk to the anonymous Russian peasant in *The Way of the Pilgrim*. I confess that I do pray the Jesus Prayer more often when I feel my human limits are reached, indicating my powerlessness rather using the prayer on God's terms. Nouwen teaches about the paradox of prayer, learning to pray when we can only receive prayer as a gift. It is God's spirit, God's breath that prays into and with us. Instead, I so often use prayer, especially the Jesus Prayer in times of weakness, as a support system, a foxhole prayer, when I no longer can help or control the situation and am desperate, a surrendering, Nouwen reminds us to use the Jesus Prayer as a prayer when we are able instead to reach out to God not on our own terms and needs but on God's terms. This kind of prayer then pulls us away from self-preoccupations, and challenges us to enter a new world, a great adventure, praying to our God who has no limits.

Nouwen's book, *Reaching Out*, about the spiritual journey and union with God using the Jesus Prayer is one I keep readily available by my bed. It is one I will recommend to those who come for spiritual direction if they ask for a book to read if they are experiencing the absence of God. Nouwen writes that God is present, but God's presence is so much beyond our human experience of being connected to God that it easily is perceived as absence. Paradoxically, God's absence is often so deeply felt that it can lead to a new sense of God's presence.

This is also a good book to use in adult studies, especially in Advent or Lent.

– Helen Bacovin, translator, *The Way of the Pilgrim and The Pilgrim Continues His Way*. Image, 1978.

–Henri Nouwen, *Reaching Out: The Three Movements of the Spiritual Life*. Image, 1975.

–Henri Nouwen, *Desert Wisdom: Sayings from the Desert Fathers*. Orbis, 1982.

Labyrinth

"Labyrinths are usually in the form of a circle with a meandering but purposeful path from the edge to the center and back again. Each has only one path, and once we make the choice to enter it, the path becomes a metaphor for our journey through life, sending us to the center of the labyrinth and then back out to the edge on the same path."

–Lauren Artress, *Walking a Sacred Path: Rediscovering the Labyrinth as a Spiritual Tool.* Riverhead Books, 1995.

Walking the labyrinth is one of the most ancient of spiritual practices, first documented in 324 on the floor of a church in Algiers. One of the most famous labyrinths was used in medieval times when Christians who could not go on the Crusades in the 12th century went to the church at Chartres, France, where there was the eleven -circuit labyrinth pattern on their church floor for a pilgrimage.

Walking the labyrinth is a form of surrender to a certain path that we trust will lead us in to the center and then back out. As we concentrate on our path, the committee in our head becomes quiet as all our energy goes to staying on the path. As our body becomes quiet as well, we reconnect to our soul, the God within. We are now on the path of healing and love and wholeness. This meditative walking spiritual exercise is especially helpful for the person who has difficulty meditating and sitting still as in centering prayer.

Labyrinths are winding paths that double back before reaching a center. It is different from a maze in that there is only one way to go. You cannot get lost. It can be a time for meditation on sacred words, scripture, or discernment as you move. You can walk, crawl, skip as you walk, but you must be considerate of other pilgrims walking the path. The Episcopal priest, Lauren Artress, was a pioneer at Grace Cathedral in San Francisco for introducing the spiritual practice in the 1990's. There are books about praying and meditating while walking the labyrinth (Camp, Geoffrion) and how to make your own labyrinth (Welch). A friend, Twyla Alexander, has written a book about her pilgrimage to walk the labyrinths in 50 states and to hear the stories of the women who created them. These are just a few of the sources for a labyrinth walk.

Choose one of these books or others or go or talk with a friend who has walked the labyrinth and try this ancient practice especially if you are one who cannot sit still and meditate. I would also like to hear from you about your experience walking the labyrinth and books you have found helpful.

Lauren Artress, *Walking a Sacred Path: Rediscovering the Labyrinth as a Spiritual Practice*. Riverhead Books, 1995.

Jill Kimberly Hartwell Geoffrion, *Christian Prayer and Labyrinth and Praying the Labyrinth*. Pilgrim Press, 2004..

Carole Ann Camp, *Praying at Every Turn: Meditations for Walking the Labyrinth*. Crossroad, 2011.

Sally Welch, *Walking the Labyrinth: A Spiritual and Practical Guide*. Canterbury, 2010.

Twyla Alexander, *Labyrinth Journeys: 50 States, 51 Stories*. Springhill, 2017.

Preparing for Holy Week

Hope Out of Shameful Acts

"In the Cross and the Lynching Tree, James Cone highlights a paradox of the gospel: out of the shameful and humiliating act of crucifixion comes hope."

–Debra J. Mumford, "Living the Word." *Christian Century,* March 14, 2018.

We drove through Montgomery, Alabama, the week before the opening of The National Memorial and Museum for Peace and Justice or better known as the Lynching Memorial and Museum. We think we caught a glimpse of it in the distance. We felt a call that we must return to Montgomery someday to visit both parts.

Between 1950 and 1877 more than 4400 African American men, women and children were lynched by being burned alive, hanged, shot, drowned, or beaten to death. The memorial structure on the center of the site is made of over 800 steel monuments, one for each county in our country where a racial lynching took place. The adjacent museum is built where there once was a former warehouse where black slaves brought in by boat or rails were imprisoned before going to the slave market.

James Cone, one of American's best-known advocates of black theology and black liberation theology, ironically died two days after the opening of this memorial and museum.

In her Good Friday message in *Christian Century,* Debra Mumford reminds us how the horrific lynching of 14-year-old Emmett Till in the Mississippi Delta in August of 1955 sparked national outrage that led Rosa Parks to move from the back to the front of the bus in Montgomery that

December. Her arrest began the 381-day Montgomery bus boycott that was a groundbreaking event in the civil rights movement.

As we are to approach Holy Week, we are to remember that the cross many of us wear is the symbol of an unjust public execution. We more often relate to the resurrection that came out of it rather than the brutal killing of an innocent man. The cross's message of resurrection is hope to all who are oppressed, but we must also remember the injustice.

The Lynching Museum and Memorial, the Good Friday services we will soon participate in will hopefully remind us of the shameful acts that did and still take place in our world. We are to remember this on Good Friday and remind each other, especially our spiritual friends, that our hope, our small part is not unlike that of Rosa Parks. We are to change the world by remembering the cruelty and standing our ground with trembling hearts in love wherever we see injustice.

Cone and Mumford are reminding us that when we talk with spiritual friends at some point we are also to remind them that our traditions teach us about great hope that can follow horrendous and unjust tragedy.

Holy Week

Which Part for Holy Week, Palm Sunday

"And many believed in him."

–John 10:31-42

We are approaching one of the holiest <u>times</u> of the Christian year, appropriately named, Holy Week. In preparing for this time, our tradition suggests the sacrament of the reconciliation of a penitent. Today, I share with you the rough draft of my confession of the ups and downs of my relationship with God looking through the lens of the Stations of the Cross that many followed this Lent as well as this upcoming Holy Week.

Today, on Palm Sunday, we will read the passion gospel in Mark, and Good Friday we will hear the passion gospel from John. Many congregations have also been reading Luke during Lent, and this week we will be reading part of that gospel's passion narrative. I imagine myself as so many of the players in this extraordinary drama. Come with me and see if you as well have a part to play. I have been Judas and betrayed Jesus for politics and money. At the same time, I have also had the privilege for seventeen years of preparing Christ's supper. Jesus has washed my feet. I have sung hymns with him on the way to mountaintops. I have publicly declared Jesus as my God in front of large groups of people. I have prayed with Christ and fallen asleep either literally or by staying unconscious to the present moment. I have figuratively cut off ears defending him in my zeal. I have been Nicodemus coming to him secretly at night and speaking out for him in ways that would keep me safe. I have given false witness against him by making my plan his plan. I have been Peter and denied my God more than three times. I have spat on him and mocked him by my actions. I have been Pilate's wife receiving dreams that tell me that God is among us. I have been Pilate and washed my hands of situations where I should have spoken out for what I knew in my heart was wrong. I have been Barabbas, the criminal who was freed, and did not have to face the consequence of my sins. I have been privileged to wipe the face of God present in so many others in pain. I have perhaps been Simon of Cyrene and carried another's cross for brief periods of time. I have been among the women who followed Jesus from Galilee and looked helplessly on his crucifixion from a distance. I have been the thief on the cross crying out for God's mercy in my distress. I have been the other thief on the cross still trying to tell God what God should do to relieve my pain. I have been the centurion at Jesus' death, finally recognizing God in the lives of so many only after they have died. I have been Joseph of Arimathea and found a resting place for him. I have been one of the spice-bearing women at the empty tomb still looking for God. I have been Mary Magdalene in the garden, searching for God and not recognizing him.

I close with an invitation to take again this Holy Week journey. I hear there is a surprise ending.

Wiederkehr: The Spaces

"Long ago when I was learning to type, I used to delight in typing letters to my friends without pressing the space bar. Now when you don' press the space bar, you've got a real mess, and there is much decoding to be done. It is the spaces in between that enable us to understand the message."

–Macrina Wiederkehr, *The Song of the Seed: A Monastic Way of Tending the Soul*. HarperOne, 1997.

I remember reading this message from Sister Wiederkehr over twenty years ago, and it still jumps off the page for me. She reminds us that many of us keep forgetting to press the space bar in our lives. She calls it hurry sickness. We will rest after we finish this one email, or project or phone call or meeting. She is calling us to spaces of contemplation or meditation or silence at intervals in our lives. One of my favorite definitions is to stop what we are doing and attend a Quaker meeting in our head. Macrina reminds us of a Native American saying, Listen or our tongue will keep us deaf! I know often when I wake up in the morning, suddenly an answer or idea about a writing comes after that long time of rest during the night. I know when I stop during the day to say prayers at daily intervals, life is more beautiful. But I can so easily become the driver of a Mack truck coming down a steep hill without brakes and hurriedly drive during the day from task to task without stopping.

Our computers and our iPhones are speaking to us. Have you ever noticed how much bigger the space bars are than the letters?

Kathleen Battle, Feinberg, Barlow, Christian Century: Sparrows

"Or not two sparrows sold for a penny? Yet not one of them will fall to the ground apart from your Father. And even the hairs of your head are all counted. So, do not be afraid: you are of more value than many sparrows."

–Matthew 10:29-31

The Christian Century: Thinking Critically, Living Faithfully is a biweekly magazine with current religious topics. I started subscribing many years ago when a Scott Lee told me Barbara Brown Taylor often wrote for it. Today I especially look for a section called "The Word, Reflections on the Lectionary" where some amazing ministers of all denominations write a response to the Sunday lectionary readings. In the June 7, 2017, issue Liddy Barlow, executive minister of Christian Associates of Southwest Pennsylvania, was the guest preacher writing about the sparrow text from Matthew for the Sunday of June 25th. She writes about the lawyer Kenneth Feinberg who chaired the September 11 Victim Compensation Fund giving money to the family of those who died in the terrorist attack using a formula depending on the income and earning potential of the victim. The compensations ranged from $250, 000 to $7.1 million. At the end of the experience, Feinberg struggles with this differentiation and wonders if one person is really 28 times more valuable than another as he personally listens to the stories of the victims and their families.

Barlow also writes of the Civilla Martin poem, "His Eye Is on the Sparrow," which became a gospel hymn bringing comfort to the African-

American church in our past century. I will never forget hearing Kathleen Battle sing this hymn a cappella with a concert of the National Symphony at the Kennedy Center. We were on the first-row center and she was there in front of us, a foot away in this striking dark red velvet dress. Her soul was singing from something deep inside of her.

This indeed is a scripture passage and a hymn about how valuable we each are to God. So often people do come for spiritual direction when they do not feel valued by God. When we talk, I so wish I could sing this song like Kathleen Battle and let them their worth.

Barlow concludes her message by telling us that Feinberg is again consulted by the president of Virginia Tech about how to distribute the fund for compensation to the families of those killed in the mass shooting there in 2007. Feinberg has been changed by his 9/11 experience and has come to believe in an equality of all life. He recommends that all victims, students and faculty receive the **same** compensation.

This is the story of how the God our understanding works in the world, a God who so desperately loves and values each and every one of us.

Experiencing Holy Week: By His Wounds

"Pay attention to what happens in the next few days. Pay attention to what goes on around you and within you. Pay attention to the water on your feet and the roughness of the towel in your hand. Pay attention to the softness of the bread and the sting of the wine in your throat. Pay attention to the brusqueness of the kiss and the splinters of the cross. Pay attention to the coldness of the tomb and the terror that clutches your heart. Pay attention to the brightness of the dawning light and the life that bursts forth."

–Br. James Koester, SSJE, from "Brother, Give Us a Word," a daily email sent to friends and followers of the Society of Saint John the Evangelist, a religious order for men in the Episcopal/Anglican Church. www.ssje.org

I remember reading this quote one Holy Week when one of my childhood wounds had been painfully opened. My "not good enough" button was pushed. As I came out of the cloud of humiliation, I read this piece about Jesus' wounds. In some very, very small way I had experienced a wound.

The "brightness of the dawning light" is indeed knowing I had been experiencing Holy Week fully with the woundedness, the sadness, the humiliation as well as the joy that I anticipated. I remember many years again another Holy Week when I had a complication from a medical procedure I performed that week. I still remember the sadness I felt for the harm I caused to my patient instead of bringing healing. I could only imagine how my patient must have felt. I realized how difficult it was and is to accept that we are human and make mistakes and accept responsibility for our mistakes.

Today I also experience life bursting worth as I try to reach out of myself and reach out to someone else I know today who has been wounded, for yesterday I was very painfully reminded what it is like. Buechner talks about what a difference it makes in our suffering knowing that Jesus not only is always beside us in our suffering, but he suffered himself as well.

We identify with Jesus. He identifies with us. We identify with others. He heals our wounds as we reach out to others. We are constantly called to community where we learn to accept our humanness, our sins and mistakes, to be forgiven, healed, loved, and blessed.

In community there is redemption and resurrection.

McCann: Seeing Jesus in Holy Week

"Or do you not know that your body is a temple of the Holy Spirit within you, whom you have from God? You are not your own."

–I Corinthians 6.19

Guest Writer: Sandra McCann
A prior musing from a village in Tanzania, "Mirror for Holy Week"

This mirror from my compact was the only one available to me for Holy Week. It was an interesting experience--not that I missed a long mirror, because I didn't. That is a great freedom for me here--never worrying about clothes or fashion. But I began to think about people who have never seen themselves and to reflect on what that must be like.

When the Maasai children look at a picture of themselves on my camera, they don't realize they are seeing themselves. The other children will say: That's you. That's you. And then they will stare hard at the picture and often break out in laughter.

I could not imagine what it would be like to not know what I looked like. I think about how much time in my life I have spent fretting in front of a mirror. How is my hair, my make-up, my clothes? These my issues are not problems in Maasai Land.

What would life without mirrors be like? Would perfect freedom come if Jesus were our only mirror?

Charleston: Recovery and Compassion

"Those who have been broken, in mind, body or spirit, who have been humbled and hurt, but have made their way back, held on and kept going, sought forgiveness and found redemption, discovered a healing they never expected, to all those who understand this experience without the need for further words, I offer this recognition: you are the sisters and brothers of compassion, the ones who know what it feels like, the ones who are witnesses to life reclaimed. Be blessed in your recovery, for each one of you is a source of faith for so many, who see in you the answer to a prayer they ask for themselves."

–Steven Charleston, Facebook Post.

So many spiritual writers continue to tell us this truth as does our own experience. We become healers of the suffering in this world because we also know the face and body of internal and external injury. This is the continual story of how Easter can follow Good Friday. Once we have experienced suffering, we can learn about, experience compassion, compassion shown to us by others who also know about wounds, as they were ministered to by others who also were wounded. This can be the cycle of compassion.

There is a choice, however. We daily live with those who live through their suffering by causing more pain to others, an "eye for an eye and a tooth for a tooth." This is the life of fear and retaliation, hurting others before they can hurt us.

Perhaps these who are so fearful were ministered to by those who never knew compassion, so they only learned about inflicting more suffering.

Perhaps we can help break their cycle by compassion, hearing their story, hoping they will share how their woundedness began. This is what spiritual friends do.

We listen to each other's story and look for sparks, compassion, the presence of God in our suffering and reminding each other that this presence is always, always there, there in people and places where we least expect it, the tears, the hug of a child, the nurse or physician or X-ray technologist who makes eye contact and holds our hand when they see our pain, the aging, crippled woman at the food pantry who tells us to have a blessed day. Our wounds can be openings for the presence of God, the great healer, in our life and the lives of others.

Buechner: Maundy Thursday

"'WHAT YOU ARE GOING to do,' Jesus says, 'do quickly.'... Jesus tells them, 'My soul is very sorrowful, even to death,' and then asks the disciples to stay and watch for him while he goes off to pray... His prayer is, 'Abba, Father, all things are possible for thee; remove this cup from me; yet not what I will but what thou wilt,'--- this tormented muddle of a prayer which Luke says made him sweat until it 'became like great drops of blood falling down upon the ground.' He went back to find some solace in the company of his friends then, but he found them all asleep when he got there. 'The spirit indeed is willing, but the flesh is weak,' he said, and you feel that it was to himself that he was saying it as well as to them."

–Frederick Buechner, "Last Supper." *The Faces of Jesus: A Life Story.* Paraclete Press, 1974.

We all so struggle with our own humanity. So many spiritual friends I meet with, including myself, spend a lifetime seeking perfection. Holy Week is a time for us specially to remember Jesus' struggle with his humanity best told in the synoptic gospels of Matthew, Mark, and Luke. On Maundy Thursday in these gospels Jesus lets us know how difficult the human condition is as he asks this cup to pass, he sweats "blood," he suffers, he cries out in anguish, he thirsts, he even asks God, "Where are you?"

A huge painting of Jesus praying at Gethsemane hung at the front of the Methodist Church where I grew up in Virginia. The image of Jesus praying in the garden is different from any of the other references in the gospels to his praying. This time scripture connects us to the human side of Jesus. This is an image to keep when we as well are praying for difficult situations in our lives.

We can talk to and identify with those who have had similar experiences to ours. I see this most in grief recovery groups where people listen to each other because they know that the other has some idea of the pain they are going through. I see this in 12-step groups where alcoholics and addicts and co-dependents listen to others who walked a very similar path to theirs. How amazing that our God loves us so much, so much that God came to be among us to let us know that God has experienced and understands what it is like to suffer and be human. There is no greater love.

Good Friday

"The courageous women who weep…"

–John 18:1-19:42

"On Good Friday, so much focus is rightfully on Jesus' suffering on the cross. But let's look down below him and see the courageous women of John's story. In memory of them, let us pray for women who today will weep for their children, refusing to be comforted. And let us hold in prayer the women on today's Golgothas who, in the face of horrible suffering, somehow find the strength to hold each other up."

–Eileen D. Crowley, "Sunday's Coming." *Christian Century,* April 11, 2017.

In Arkansas last year starting on Easter Monday there were eleven executions planned because one of the drugs being used had an expiration date at the end of that month. There had not been an execution for twelve years. I remember that earlier execution well because I was a deacon at our cathedral then which is close to the governor's mansion. We had an ecumenical prayer service for the person to be executed and the person he killed. I know I played the harp at the service, probably the African American spiritual, "Sometimes I Feel Like a Motherless Child." We then went to the governor's mansion and sang and prayed by candlelight until after the execution.

All of the men on death row last year had killed young women. I wonder what these girls now in eternal life are praying for and if they are lighting candles. Some of the stories about the men reveal that they had awful lives with a lack of love from women like the ones who followed Jesus. My prayers today are of course that governors all over our country will stay executions and that eventually this state could abolish the death penalty.

My third prayer is that we will do our best to raise strong and loving women like the ones at the cross with Jesus so that their children will know love and not violence against others, especially against women.

Easter Vigil 1

"Dear friends in Christ: On this most holy night, in which our Lord Jesus passed over from death to life, the Church invites her members, dispersed throughout the world, to gather in vigil and prayer."

—*Book of Common Prayer*

For the church, the Easter Vigil is one of the most complicated and beautiful services of the year. The difficulty is that it is only once a year so it is hard to remember all the tiny details from year to year, so sometimes there is more chaos than the church would like. But this is also what adds to its beauty, light and creation coming out of chaos. The service starts with the lighting of the pascal candle from a fire, usually outside of the church and its entering inside into the church in complete darkness.

The deacon carries the pascal candle in as he or she lights the congregation's candles while singing, "The Light of Christ", three times, each time a little higher pitch. This is followed by the deacon chanting the beautiful Exsultet.

It is time for me to turn the Exsultet over to someone else. I have loved chanting the Exsultet for over seventeen years. It has been a privilege. A newer deacon singing the Exsultet this year has been practicing it for two years and so lovingly and beautifully chants it from her heart. The Exsultet is followed by Old Testament readings about God's history with God's people. Next come baptisms, crying babies, curious toddlers escaping from their parents still in the dark. Finally, the cacophony of the great noise of bells of every size announce that Christ has risen indeed as all the lights come on, and we see all the flowers of

Easter surrounding the inside of the church. Then we celebrate the first new Eucharist of the Easter season.

The service may have some similarity to what the spice bearing women experienced when they came to the empty tomb on that early Easter morning and saw one or two angels in dazzling white telling them that they were the first to know that Jesus had been raised from the dead!

Easter Week and Beyond

Nouwen: Easter Message

"When you forget your true identity as a beloved child of God, you lose your way in life."

–Henri Nouwen, "Holy Saturday/ Easter Vigil, Be Not Afraid." *From Fear to Love: Lenten Reflections on the Parable of the Prodigal Son*, Creative Communications of the Parish, 2009.

So many spiritual friends I talk with so well understand Nouwen's Easter message to us. For a multitude of reasons, often fear based, we lose our true identity. We forget that we are loved by God and seek love everywhere else. We stop becoming the person God created us to be and become the person others or our society want us to be. We become people pleasers, fearing rejection. We become insecure, fearful, frightened and look for relief in power, addictions, fame, money, attachments to others and become dependent on what others think about us, or we may become paralyzed and unable to make any decisions. We eventually become very aware that we have lost our connection to God. Where can we find help?

My experience is that it is in community where we are helped. We talk with others who can share their connection to God. In recovery groups this is known as "sticking with the winners," "staying close to those who still have their lights on." Eventually we are healed, and we stay connected by reaching out to others in need who have gone through a similar experience.

As the alcoholic or addict in recovery stays sober and clean by sharing his or her story, we talk to someone else who is seeking recovery and tell them our story of Resurrection from Good Friday.

Some may not call it Easter, but that is what it is. I was reminded of this by a dear friend, Jim Waldron, who now lives in the resurrection, who indeed did become sober on Easter Sunday many years ago.

The Child in Us

"Whoever does not receive the kingdom of God as a little child will never enter it. And he took them up in his arms, laid his hands on them, and blessed them."

–Mark 10:15-16

I was born on Easter Sunday. My name is Joanna. My parents had intended to name me Jo Anna after my mother's parents, Joe and Anna. Before my mother woke up from her anesthesia at my birth my father put Jo and Anna together and added in a middle name, Marie. This is a statement about my parent's relationship, which most probably began before my birth. Marie was my father's favorite sister who was married the day before I was born. My father missed most of the wedding celebration because of my impending arrival, so I guess I was his wedding present to his sister!

The first Easter I remember is in a picture that I keep as a sacred place on my desk. It is the Easter before my brother was born, so I must have been barely two years old. I am standing in front of our first house by the Mattaponi River at the corner of Second and Lee Streets. The screened in front porch is in the background with maybe an Easter basket on it. There is a scruffy shrub to my right side. My head barely reaches the floor of the screened in porch. The small photograph is in black and white, and the silver from the photograph over the years has transformed the clear plastic cover to a grayish yellow color, leaving parts of the picture mystically missing and other parts without as much light, giving the photograph an overall Easter film noir look. I think the woven brim hat I am wearing is white with a black ribbon around it. My memory is that the coat I am wearing is a light pink wool with fake pockets, and big buttons. The coat falls not quite evenly just above my knees. I am sure that one of my sweet grandmothers made my Easter coat. My left shoulder looks slightly higher than the right. The tips of my hands are barely seen, sheltered under the coat as my arms stand straight almost at attention by my side. I am wearing a little homemade corsage on my left lapel. I cannot make out the flower, but I think it may be a small rose. Circling my neck and overlapping the coat is a ruffled white collar with a small black bow that must be the top of my homemade dress that is otherwise in secret beneath my coat. I cannot see my feet, but my legs are looking good. My eyes are wide open and my straight blonde hair has been curled, most probably with toilet paper the night before. I have a look of serene panic on my face as if I do not know what will happen next, but I will be ready.

This picture has become my inner child. I long to meet her once again someday. For right now I keep her by my side always on my desktop right next to my Apple, trying to let her know all is well, no harm will come to her. It is Easter, a celebration of new life overcoming death. She will never ever be abandoned again. We will go shopping for her new Easter outfit. I will tell her the Easter story and remind her how much she is loved. I will bring her flowers, violets or tulips or daffodils, go to an Easter egg hunt with her, give her a noisy gong to ring at the Easter Vigil, gather more flowers for her, maybe azaleas from our backyard, to flower the cross on Easter Day, ask her if she would like to sing with the other children at the Easter Day service, secretly leave for her a little extra chocolate at the Easter Brunch, rest with her in the afternoon, play with her the next day on Easter Monday, maybe even go to a movie. She is my inner child, born on Easter Sunday. I will remind her that Easter Day next year will again be a celebration of her birthday. Her real name is Jo Anna, and she is very loved especially by those whose name she wears.

John Updike: Short Easter

"The fact that the day is Easter means something to him–something he can neither name nor get out of his mind."

–John Updike, "Short Easter." *The Afterlife and Other Stories*, Alfred A. Knopf, Inc. and The Penguin Group, 1994. Originally in *The New Yorker*, Match 19, 1989.

John Updike has written one of my favorite resurrection short stories in *The Afterlife and Other Short Stories* called "Short Easter" about the occasion when daylight saving time begins on Easter Sunday. I first read the story in Volume 2 of *Listening for God*, a series of short stories selected by Paula Carlson and Peter Hawkins, the first then from the department of English and the second a professor of Religion and Literature, both at Yale University. The four-part series includes a DVD about the author of each contemporary short story which can be studied especially in a book group to use literature as an icon to hear and see God.

In "Short Easter," this high holy day for Christians becomes one hour shorter when the clocks are jumped forward and an hour of sleep is stolen. "Church bells rang in the dark." Updike goes through the day of a well to do man named Fogel ("Fog" is God spelled backwards). who keeps wanting to attend church services on Easter Day but puts it off until at the end of the day, he has never gone. At the story's end, Fogel wakes up from an afternoon nap "amid that unnatural ache of resurrection. the weight of coming again to life" and realizes that "although everything in his world is in place, there is something immensely missing."

This is the moment of clarity that God continuously reveals to us. I regularly need to remind myself and spiritual friends to try to be open to that moment that is often fearful as it was for Fogel. It is like the fear of the women at the empty tomb on Easter Day. It is resurrection. It always speaks to something more that we have missed.

We have put something else in our "God hole," and whatever it is, prestige, money, marriage, work, family, fame, beauty, it will never fill that hole inside of us where only God is large enough to live.

Easter Week Visits

"For I am convinced that neither death, nor life, nor angels, nor rulers, nor things present, nor things to come, nor powers, nor height, nor depth, nor anything else in all creation, will be able to separate us from the love of God in Christ Jesus our Lord."

–Romans 8:38-39

I talk with so many people who do not believe they deserve God's love. I remember visiting with a very alert, highly educated woman in her 90's still involved in her successful business who wanted to start going back to church but only after she got her life back together and felt like she was a better person. I told her the famous line that "the church is not a museum for saints but a hospital for sinners," but she never returned.

I talk to many people recovering from addiction who feel so much shame for the life they have led. They do not see how God and others can forgive them. So many have been raised by a judgement God who is looking over their shoulder to catch them in sin.

I want to let them know that there is another way, those who believe in resurrection, an Easter, which always can come after a Good Friday life or experience. If I can, I remind them of Jesus' disciples who abandoned, denied him. He did not return to them in that upper room on Easter evening and say, "Shame on you." Instead he said, "'Peace be with you.' When he had said this, he breathed on them and said to them. 'Receive the Holy Spirit. If you forgive the sins of any, they are forgiven'" (John 20).

We talk about the difference between shame, "I am a bad person," and guilt, "I did a wrong thing." We also talk about addictions not being a moral failing, but a disease.

We talk about seeing any sign of God's love alive and well, working in their life. We pray that the Holy Spirit will led both of us to recognize the Spirit alive in each other, to see and be led by the Christ in each other. Sometimes I tell my story of how God has been present in my life through so many difficulties to see if they see any similarity in my story and theirs. Lastly, I may share the above mantra from Romans I used for several years as I became more aware of the harm I had done in my life to others and myself and was seeking forgiveness.

Easter Vigil 2

"How blessed is this night when earth and heaven are joined and man is reconciled to God."

—Book of Common Prayer

I revisit this past Holy Week and remember some wonderful stories of the excitement of the Easter Vigil at each of the churches where I have served. I remember one priest telling us at his homily many years ago that our presence at the Vigil didn't give us extra points with God for being there, getting more stars in our crown. It was simply a privilege to be some of the first at the empty tomb to meet the risen Lord.

One of my favorite surprises was waiting to see how the altar guild would often decorate my larger harp for the Easter Vigil.

Many congregations then follow the Vigil service with an elaborate reception or dinner late at night at church or at someone's home.

Once at Trinity Cathedral as the deacon tilted the candle ever so slightly to light its wick from the first fire, oil ran out of the top of the candle and the fire became surreal, like the tongues of fire described at Pentecost. At St. Margaret's we did the Vigil in the Columbarium garden and I played a smaller lap harp as I sang the Exsultet to stay on key. I cannot describe the feeling of shouting out in the great outdoors, "The Lord has risen indeed!

At St. Luke's one of my favorite lectors reading one of the Old Testament lessons was having difficulty seeing in the dark in the middle of the long reading and put her candle closer to the microphone at the lectern catching the foam covering over the microphone on fire. She so elegantly blew the fire out and didn't miss a beat in the reading. Also, at St. Luke's one of the amazing teachers of the children ministries and her two children planned a flashlight egg hunt for older children after the Vigil outside around the church which was a huge success as well as increasing the number of young people at the service!

The Vigil is so unusual, however, that it also is so easy to get caught up in the many tiny details of this once a year liturgy and view it as a performance rather than an offering. The Vigil is a service to be enjoyed and celebrated. We can always count on the Vigil to bring surprises just like the risen Lord.

Myrrh Bearers

"But on the first day of the week, at early dawn, they came to the tomb, taking the spices that they had prepared."

–Luke 24:1

I am preparing for a workshop for the International Community of Hope conference this summer in Texas. Community of Hope began out of a need to train those who are not ordained to be hospital chaplains at St. Luke's Hospital in Houston. The training is now used all over the world for people interested in visiting the sick and homebound. I have been involved in the Community of Hope in our diocese for over twenty years and continue to see it as outstanding preparation and study for people who are called to any ministry that involves pastoral care. One of the hallmarks of the training is that it is steeped in Benedictine spirituality.

The image of the Community of Hope Chaplains that keeps coming to me is that of the myrrh bearers, the women who brought spices to the tomb of Jesus on that early Easter morning. They brought their most precious possessions to honor the one who had cared for them. My experience is that this has also been the story for many of the people who are called to the ministry of pastoral care. They know what it is like to be wounded, and they have been ministered to by other healers. They know what it is like to be loved and cared for by others. Their only way of sharing and continuing and keeping that love is to carry what they have learned to someone else.

What happens with their visit is something totally unexpected. They go to honor their friend and teacher and instead they are promised a new life, a resurrection in this life and the next.

I have never experienced a visit where I did not receive resurrection. We are touched and healed by those we go to visit. We take our most precious possessions, ourselves, our time, our presence and make an offering. In return we always meet the resurrected Christ in so many forms.

Nouwen: Crushed Grapes

"Sometimes our sorrow overwhelms us so much that we no longer can believe in joy. Life just seems a cup filled to the brim with war, violence, rejection, loneliness, and endless disappointments. At times like this we need our friends to remind us that crushed grapes can produce tasty wine."

–Henri Nouwen, "April 7." *Bread for the Journey,* HarperOne, 1997.

Our God does not promise that we will not experience sorrow or tragedy, but God does promise that God will be with us through our despair and that out of every Good Friday experience comes a resurrection, an Easter. When we, our friends, or those we come to comfort are in the middle of sorrow and pain, these words are not comforting. We are called at first to be the love of God just by our presence to those who grieve. There are not words to comfort, only our love and presence, which can be a healing presence.

As the sorrow eases, we can slowly give this promise of an Easter experience where crushed grapes turn into wine. I see people whose son committed suicide develop programs for suicide prevention so that others will not have to go through their experience. I see those who have experienced the death of a loved one now be the first ones to reach out to others whose loved one has died and just go and sit beside them for hours. Parents whose child has been killed in a tragic accident build a playground or a trail so that other children will have a safe place to go. A family whose teenage daughter dies in a car accident begins a program for the arts for teens in public schools since art made such a difference in their daughter's life. A group who develop a friendship in a grief recovery group develop a funeral team at their church to care for families before, during, and after the service.

All of us are a product of our wounds. We have a choice. We can learn and work and live through our wounds and over time at some point experience another Easter and taste a new wine, or we can stay isolated and buried in our Good Friday tomb. My experience is that Christ stays there with us as long as it takes, ready to roll away the stone as new life emerges.

Chant Exsultet Easter

"Chant calls us out of chronological time, in which 'now' can never be located, and into the eternal now, which is not really found in time."

–David Steindl-Rast, *The Music of Silence: Entering the Sacred Space of Monastic Experience*. HarperOne, 1995.

David Steindl-Rast reminds us that when we use this ancient voice in praising and praying to God and speaking to each other we are standing in the presence of ancient angel choirs. We are changing the way we address God and each other. The words become notes. The message we chant sounds different. The sounds of chant are soothing, comforting. The music takes us to another place and another time. The sounds open our world to another dimension. Chanting slows down the words of the message. The squirrels running in the cage in our head slow down and become a bit quieter. Sometimes time seems to stand still, and we feel at peace. We are home.

The chant that deacon's most often sing is the Exsultet which follows bringing the newly lighted Christ candle back into the church at the Easter Vigil. Even before Lent begins, this music becomes part of my body even if I am not the deacon designated to sing this lengthy canticle. Jason Pennington, the music director at one of my previous churches, describes the Exsultet as "one of the most difficult chants of the Church's treasury of song, sung at the opening of the Great Vigil, at the culmination of the events of the holy triduum as all of the congregation is holding their candles in the shadow of the one Paschal, the choir not yet allowed into the stalls, standing in the nave with the faithful as that most beautiful of canticles is intoned, the Exsultet, promising us all the immeasurable gift of salvation."

I keep a note from Jason from our last Easter together when I was having some mobility issues and standing for a length of time was more difficult. "She was facing excruciating physical pain to stand for the lengthy canticle as she drew each breath to acclaim its message of life. She paced it well, taking her time and savoring every single phrase as if it were the very first. This was a beautiful gift of ministry, a Holy Spirit gift that put ministry before self. And isn't that exactly the lesson to have been learned at the Mandatum not two nights before: 'I give you a new commandment, that you should love one another.' Joanna's lovely, quiet chanting voice was tremulous with pain, yet was filled with joy. This was Easter."

I keep Jason's note to help remind me and others that chanting is always an offering, never a performance. The chant that deacon's most often sing is the Exsultet which follows bringing the newly lighted Christ candle back into the church at the Easter Vigil. Even before Lent begins, this music becomes part of my body even if I am not the deacon designated to sing this lengthy canticle. Jason Pennington, the music director at one of my previous churches, describes the Exsultet as "one of the most difficult chants of the Church's treasury of song, sung at the opening of the Great Vigil, at the culmination of the events of the holy triduum as all of the congregation is holding their candles in the shadow of the one Paschal, the choir not yet allowed into the stalls, standing in the nave with the faithful as that most beautiful of canticles is intoned, the Exsultet, promising us all the immeasurable gift of salvation."

I keep Jason's note to help remind me and others that chanting is always an offering, never a performance.

Kelsey: The Ballard of Judas Iscariot

"We forget that the real task is to bring the totality of our psychic being to God and not just to repress and split off those parts of ourselves that we cannot change."

–Morton T. Kelsey, *The Other Side of Silence: A Guide to Christian Meditation.* Paulist Press, 1976.

Theologian, Morton Kelsey wrote a very practical book over fifty years ago called *The Other Side of Silence, a Guide to Christian Meditation* to remind Christians that meditation was not just for those in Eastern religions. His revised edition twenty years later is called *The Other Side of Silence, Meditation for the Twenty-first Century* has more of his writings and wisdom in a time when Christian meditation now is more well-known. Kelsey believes that meditation is simply the way we set up the conditions to prepare for the God who is seeking us and breaks through to us particularly in silence. "Doing meditation" involves using Biblical stores, dream images, poems, images from other sources.

Included in Kelsey's book is a moving poem, "The Ballad of Judas Iscariot," by the Scottish poet, Robert Buchanan, which I always read and meditate on every Easter season, reminding us that no one is lost or not forgiven or not loved by God. The ballad must have been powerful to hear it sung. The story is of Judas wandering through regions of darkness when he spies a light from a lantern at a doorway. Jesus is holding up the light as he beckons to Judas to come in and join his fellow disciples getting ready to eat. Jesus tells Judas they were just waiting for him before pouring the wine.

I offer the poem also to spiritual friends who feel they have done something unforgivable or that God no longer loves them, and of course I meditate on it myself when that darkness of guilt or shame or a poor self-image surrounds me as well. Judas is a reminder and icon of times when we cannot accept that we might be forgiven or loved or might be open to God's Grace continuously offered to all of us through dark and light times in our life. In all honestly, was Judas' betrayal of Jesus really worse than denying Jesus or abandoning him as the others did? Judas simply could not ask for or accept forgiveness and had forgotten that the God of his understanding was a loving and forgiving God.

Resurrection

"Our memory of Jesus' resurrection fails us if we only understand his resurrection as a miracle. Jesus' resurrection was indeed a miracle; however, Jesus' resurrection needs to be more than a miracle. It's needs to be normal... every day... how we live and breathe: with resurrection power."

–Br. Curtis Almquist, SSJE, from "Brother, Give Us a Word," a daily email sent to friends and followers of the Society of Saint John the Evangelist, a religious order for men in the Episcopal/Anglican Church. www.ssje.org

This is at the heart of spiritual direction, helping spiritual friends see daily, yearly resurrection in their lives in the daily, yearly Good Fridays that present themselves. It often does take more than three days to be aware of these resurrections. As we become more conscious of the resurrections, we become more open to trust and be a little more patient that there will be a resurrection out of each new darkness we face.

My experience also is that I most often draw closer, spend more time with God during the darkness. In the dark Good Fridays of my life is where I learn about surrender, where I "re-turn" my life and my will over to God.

A close family member or friend dies. We learn about the sacredness of life and spend more time living in the present with gratitude for each day. We learn to honor and be grateful for the relationship we had by extending the love and kindness we learned in that relationship to others.

Our children act out. We see our part in it and try to change our relationship with them.

Our job becomes more and more difficult. We finally leave it or maybe are even fired. After much time we find a job that is our bliss.

A medical illness slows us down. We learn about a more meaningful life at a slower pace living a day at a time.

We are caught in our addiction and lose our job. We change our whole live-style and outlook on life in order to live without the addiction.

Someone has harmed us mentally, physically, or spiritually. Over much time we realize that unless we can forgive them and move on, they are still hurting us. We then slowly learn about daily forgiveness for the small hurts we feel each day.

Miracles that become the ordinary. God at work in our lives.

Sue Monk Kidd: Incubation in Darkness

"Today (August 12) is my birthday. It makes me think of the new life I'm incubating and the Birth-day still to come. Today I'll talk to myself. I'll say, 'Accept life-the places it bleeds and the places it smiles. That's your most holy and human task. Gather up the pain and the questions and hold them like a child up your lap. Have faith in God, in the movement of your soul. Accept what is. Accept the dark. It's okay. Just be true.'"

–Sue Monk Kidd, "A Journal Entry." *When the Heart Waits: Spiritual Direction for Life's Sacred Questions,* HarperOne, 1992.

Today we continue to share stories from author, Sue Monk Kidd.

I found two copies of Sue Monk Kidd's book, *When the Heart Waits: Spiritual Direction for Life's Sacred Questions* unread, in my home library. When I saw the book on the list for my spiritual direction studies at the Haden Institute, I took it as a sign to read it. I still remember the first time I met Sue Monk Kidd. She was on a tour for her book, *The Dance of the Dissident Daughter.* I took all of my female partners in my medical group and my daughter to hear her. One of my partners cried the entire time and bought several books.

Kidd is as amazing as a speaker as she is as a writer. Kidd reminds us of Marian Woodman's writings about creative suffering in the dark. Creative suffering burns clean as opposed to neurotic suffering that creates more soot. Creative suffering "easters" us or transforms us, chooses a new way, owns our shadow, heals our wounds, as opposed to neurotic or self-pitying suffering which is un-transforming and leads to despair. Kidd continues to tell us that pain may not kill us but running from it might.

She describes a healing exercise at a retreat she led at Kanuga where they all put on the altar cut up scrapes of colored papers representing wounds and pain from their lives, offering them up, turning them over instead pushing them down, trying to escape from them.

She reminds us that the most significant events in Jesus' life occurred in darkness: birth, arrest, death, resurrection. As tiny bits of light come out in our lives, we begin eastering just like the lighting of the Pascal candle at the Easter Vigil. This is a great image for me, for the deacon usually carries the Pascal candle saying "the light of Christ" three times and then sings the Exsultet, praising the light. The Pascal candle at our church is real wax and for some reason is always very difficult to extinguish!

Kidd describes how our addictions keep us unaware of what is going on inside of us as well as outside of us. This reminds me of when I am living in my addiction, I keep my mind and my body from feeling the harm to my body and soul and heart that comes from wearing my many false selves that we talked about yesterday. Twenty-seven years ago, when I was introduced to a 12-step program, I got my voice back, but the recovery in the darkness of dealing with the tensions of all the false selves is still part of my recovery as I try to live the steps. More and more I can see easterings or resurrection, but it is still hard work. When the true self emerges, there is delight in life. Gratitude is what the true self of life brings. God becomes our playmate and we find our inner child.

Kidd writes about our accelerated, instant, quick "fast-food" society. I remember once talking to a 10-year-old about playing chess, and her response was, "It takes too long."

Kidd reminds us of our desire for shortcut religion as well, looking for what Bonhoeffer called cheap grace, "Long on butterflies but short on cocoons."

I go down to our den this afternoon and find my husband and our 11-year-old grandson quietly playing chess. I feel hope.

Sue Monk Kidd: More Incubation

"Remember that little flame on the Easter candle. Cup your heart around it. Your darkness will become the light."

–Sue Monk Kidd, "A Journal Entry." *When the Heart Waits: Spiritual Direction for Life's Sacred Questions*, HarperOne, 1992.

We continue our visit with Sue Monk Kidd. I wish I could have Sue Monk Kidd's book *When the Heart Waits: Spiritual Direction for Life's Sacred Questions* with me all the time and just read from it when I meet with other spiritual friends. I hope I can remember her message about waiting. I hope to share her ideas about the false self at the appropriate time. I see many people coming for direction on or getting ready for the "night sea journey" of biblical waiters like Jonah in the belly of the whale, or like Christ in the tomb, or like Joseph in the well. I hope to remember Kidd's phrase when we are having difficulty letting go, "Put on your courage suit" or the image of letting go like crossing a bridge.

I began this book on Maundy Thursday in the Chapel of Repose with the reserved sacrament. I am ending it in Greece with my husband, my daughter, and her husband in the week of Easter 4 as we overlook the Acropolis. I know Kidd's later books are about her trips to Greece especially with her daughter where she becomes even more connected to the feminine part of herself and God. My daughter and I have just this month published a book together just as Kidd and her daughter did. Kidd ends this book telling about a drawing which came from her true inner self of a sketch she made at Kanuga, the home of my spiritual direction class, of a mother and child. So much serendipity.

This past Sunday, on Mother's Day we dedicated a sculpture of mother and child that my husband had purchased in the garden next to St. Luke's chapel. I will attach a picture of the sculpture. More connections.

So, this week as we travel in Greece I will try to follow Kidd's direction and stay in the moment and feed my soul real food instead of junk food and see what else might happen to help me see the God within each person I meet and in myself as I continue to study to become a spiritual director and friend.

The real food I am looking for is silence, laughter, solitude, taking care of my body, swimming, massage, deep encounters, prayer, writing, reading, Eucharist, gratitude, seeing serendipity, delight, compassion, living in the present, empathy (sharing pain), and a reverence for the earth, especially in this ancient part of the earth that I will visit on land and on sea this week.

Charleston: Being Resilient and La La Land

"Life is hard. The losses, the sudden arrival of illness, the struggles within families, the pressure of a world trying to find a reason to hope. If it is to endure the gale force winds of chance, faith must be deeply rooted, anchored in trust, strengthened by courage, able to bend but never break. So here is a prayer for all of you living in the real world: may you find your faith as tough as you are and as resilient as the love that keeps you going."

–Bishop Steven Charleston, Facebook Post.

I think of the end of 2017 Academy awards when Warren Beatty couldn't understand what was in the envelope to announce the best picture of the year and handed the confusing envelope to Faye Dunaway who saw the name *La La Land* and announced that movie as the winner. They had been given the wrong envelope! It was the one announcing Emma Stone as best actress from *La La Land* that had been reported earlier. The producers and cast of *La La Land* were so excited and came up and thanked so many people. Men with headsets scurried on stage and handed Jordan Horowitz, one of the *La La Land* producers the correct envelope as he announces, "I'm sorry, No. There's a mistake. *Moonlight*, you guys won best picture!"

I will always remember the grace at which Horowitz gave up his Oscar. His whole team on stage, his dream suddenly crushed, years of hoping to win, his Oscar now being handed over to another movie producer before a live television audience in front of millions of people. Later Horowitz said to Adele Romanski, a *Moonlight* producer, "I got to give a speech and then give you an award!"

When I think of resilience, I will remember and tell his story. I think of all the mistakes I have been involved in, taking my family, particularly my husband for granted, failing to speak to a patient's family because I was too busy; all the mistakes I fear, reading the wrong gospel, preaching the wrong lessons, not chanting well, running out of bread at the Eucharist, forgetting to visit someone who then dies; all the frustration dreams of going to take a test for a class I had not attended or studied for. Knowing that a time-honored institution such as the accounting firm of PricewaterhouseCoopers can make such a mistake somehow helps me forgive myself for my own failings. This firm which has overseen the Oscar ballots for eighty-three years also was gracious, making amends for their mistake, apologizing for their human error. Human errors are part of the human condition. Forgiveness and making amends are at the heart of resilience.

When spiritual friends ask about forgiveness, we always return to Desmond and Mpho Tutu's outstanding book, *The Book of Forgiving*, where they also talk about forgiving yourself by admitting your mistake, making amends as those in 12-step recovery do. We now have role models who have forgiven others for great injustices such as Nelson Mandela in South Africa who forgive his captors for his 18 years in prison. We have the Amish community in Nickel Mines, Pennsylvania who forgave the gunman who killed five of their children and critically wounded five others on October 2, 2006. Forgiveness and amends can transform guilt and shame and anger and revenge and resentment into resilience and even more. Resurrection.

Peace of God

"Jesus doesn't offer peace of mind. He offers the peace of reconciliation."

–Diane Roth, "Living the Word." *Christian Century*, March 14, 2018.

This response by Diane Roth to Lectionary Readings for the Second Sunday in Easter from John 20:19-31 is another wake-up call for us to reconcile with those with whom we are having difficulty, loving that neighbor who is so different, loving our relatives who look at our political scene wearing a very different pair of glasses, seeing Christ in the most unlovable person with whom we work, loving those whose belief systems are the exact opposite of ours. I could go on for several more pages of examples.

A verse that haunts me that is often said at the offertory is Matthew 5:23-24, "So when you are offering your gift at the altar, if you remember that your brother or sister has something against you, leave your gift there before the altar and go; first be reconciled to your brother or sister, and then come and offer your gift."

Family systems models tells us that we must make every possible attempt to get back into relationship with any family members from whom we are estranged.

The heart of 12-step recovery is looking at the resentments we have for others, seeing our part causing the estrangement from others, making amends, seeing how we are alike instead of seeing our differences.

All of these teachings are reminding us that when we cannot love our neighbor, it is hard to love God, for the God of our understanding always also lives in our neighbor as does God live in us.

This is an important message for us to share with spiritual friends. We may not be the trained person to help our friends reconcile with those with whom they are having difficulty, but we are called to share our experience that reconciliation with our neighbor is a straight pathway to the peace of God.

Koinonia

"All who believed were together and had all things in common; they would sell their possessions and goods and distribute the proceeds to all, as any had need."

–Acts 2: 44-45

In her brilliant sermon this morning, June 3, 2018, Patricia Matthews reminds us of the winning word in this year's Scripps National Spelling Bee this weekend: Koinonia.

You can read Patricia's sermon online at St. Mark's Episcopal Church, Little Rock website and listen and see it on St. Mark's Facebook page. Fourteen-year-old Karthik Nemmani from McKinney, Texas, correctly spells this word of Greek origin meaning Christian fellowship or communion with God, especially with other Christians in community. Patricia reminds us that this 91st National Spelling Bee with the 515 participants who qualified was televised on none other than ESPN, a sport's network where we more often watch football or basketball or baseball or soccer!

When I heard the winning word this weekend and today from Patricia, my heart skipped a beat. Koinonia has been on my heart for almost a week. Our oldest granddaughter recently graduated from high school and is headed to the University of Georgia. I have been praying about how I can support her in this decision. It came as I was reading a review of two book about Clarence Jordon in *Christian Century.* I want to remind Langley about Mr. Jordon, who is perhaps one of the most outstanding graduates of the University of Georgia. His competency in Greek led him to his

"Cotton Patch" version of the New Testament as he attempted to translate the Bible into everyday language. Jordon also founded Koinonia Farm as a farming community of believers sharing their lives and resources following the example of the first Christian communities. Out of this movement came Habitat for Humanity International by Millard Fuller and later The Fuller Center for Housing as well as Jubilee partners and much support for the Civil Rights Movement.

Today after church a group of women met to begin discernment of a Daughters of the King Chapter at St. Mark's, another group seeking koinonia, fellowship with other women seeking a deeper spirituality and relationship to God through prayer, service, and evangelism.

I am going to keep koinonia on my heart for a few more days and see if I observe any more serendipitous connections or synchronicity in our world.

Charleston: Learning to read the Spiritual Signs

"You have seen the signs around you for some time now. You are beginning to understand which way the wind is blowing. The spiritual life is not an exercise of imagination, but of interpretation. We see the signs. It is understanding them as a coherent message that takes skill. The handwriting on the wall tells us nothing unless we have learned to read."

–Bishop Steven Charleston, Facebook Post.

"Learning to read the signs on the wall." Bishop Charleston is indeed giving us a good metaphor for living and discerning the spiritual life. As spiritual friends, we help each other see where God is working in our lives. We have friends helping us connect the dots, suggesting that a storm may be coming when we miss the signs. We are called to remember how God led us in our past. We have seen the signs in the past. When one of us cannot presently see the signs of God alive in our lives, those of us who can see, help out each other. This is why God calls us to community. We cannot do this alone. All of our spiritual exercises, prayer, contemplation, study, centering prayer, the labyrinth, a rosary, intentional walking, are all tools to help us interpret the handwriting on the wall, the hand of God caring for us, leading us, never abandoning us. Some spiritual disciplines we do by ourselves, others such as corporate worship we do together. Whether we experience these disciplines alone or together we are called to share what we learn with each other. Discernment for where we should go or the action to take next is most effectively done in community.

I do have friends who sit alone and meditate and say they hear where God is working in their lives and what they should do. All the better for them. I could never do this except on very rare occasions. My experience is that others can see signs I have missed while the course of action I should take is so apparent to them. All of this of course does involve a great deal of trust.

Tilden Edwards: Spiritual Direction and the Soul

"We begin with the edge of mystery, because anything coming to us from the beyondness of God has an origin that is deeper than our minds can take us. The beginning of our experience thus is shrouded in darkness."

–Tilden Edwards, "How Do We Know? The Nature of Spiritual Experience." *Spiritual Director: Spiritual Companion Guide to Tending the Soul*, Paulist Press, 2001.

The founder of the Shalem Institute for Spiritual Formation shares with us his teaching and experience as a Spiritual Director and Spiritual Companion for over a quarter century. Edwards takes us on a journey with him in his book about how spiritual companionship evolved, the nature of the soul, the nature of the spiritual experience, the nurture of the Soul, recognizing a spiritual companion, practical aspects of being in spiritual companionship, being in a spiritual relationship with the communities in which we live, and his perceived future for spiritual direction.

Edwards believes that our true identity and being is our soul. He shares his longtime experience of how our soul might interact with another. The site and fruit of this interaction is love.

Edwards seems to put "skin" on the Soul. He makes the soul become more real, enticing all of us with a longing and a deep yearning to begin to connect to the Soul not only in our neighbors but ourselves.

Edwards describes an "empty experience," the "expansions of emptiness," as an expansion of the soul. Emptiness is not the absence of God: it is simply experiencing God in a way with which we are not familiar. We are experiencing God emptied of our normal ways of understanding the spiritual experience.

Edwards: Spiritual Direction and the Soul, More

"Whatever we can know at the deepest place we know not through our cognitive thinking but through our spiritual hearts (the subtly conscious dimension of our souls) or through the even greater immediacy of our contemplative intuition (our capacity for direct, unitive involvement)."

–Tilden Edwards, "How Do We Know? The Nature of Spiritual Experience." *Spiritual Director: Spiritual Companion Guide to Tending the Soul*, Paulist Press, 2001.

As Edwards talks about the difference between the spirituality of men and women, I suddenly looked into the spiritual life of my father who loved duck hunting, not for the killing but to be in the marsh. That was one of his last wishes before he died, to go once more to the marsh. All my life I never thought of him as a spiritual being, but now I see it.

In Edward's section of the nature of the soul he describes four levels of knowing the Sprit's presence, an outer interpretive level of knowing, a little deeper descriptive knowing, then deeper heart knowing, and finally at our inner self is immediate knowing.

Edwards reminds us that it is the Soul that does the work of direction and that we are to learn to seek and follow the Soul in a spiritual companion rather than staying with a set plan we may have in mind that may not necessarily come from the Soul. The advantage of a spiritual companion is that there are now at least two Souls longing to be loved and heard, and to teach and spread love with each other and beyond.

Edwards offers many very practical ways to listen and be open to a spiritual companion that could be useful individually or with spiritual friends. When the workplace is mentioned, we can ask if there is any object at the workplace which reminds the spiritual friend of God's presence? At times a spiritual director can ask if there are others who are spiritually supporting the spiritual friend besides the director?

Edwards challenges us to be more aware of the Soul in ourselves and in our neighbor and be more aware of the love and peace that comes when Souls meet.

A Week with Margaret Guenther

Margaret Guenther I

"Let all guests who arrive be received like Christ, for He is going to say, "I came as a guest and you received Me..."

—The Rule of Saint Benedict.

This line from *The Rule of Saint Benedict* opens the first chapter of Margaret Guenther's book, *Holy Listening: The Art of Spiritual Direction.* The title could so easily have been *Practical Spiritual Direction for Clergy and Lay.* Her writing describes very practical wisdom about being a spiritual director with illustrations from her experience and biblical stories. She says her book is for the "beginner," but I have kept her writings at my desk at all times for years. At her writing in 1992, Guenther was one of the few women doing and writing about spiritual direction. Her feminine wisdom adds a new way of talking about direction, allowing the director to self-disclosure or sharing parts of her life when appropriate (as opposed to therapy). After a short "catch up time," she begins the session with silence, asking the spiritual friend to let her know when she or he is ready. She ends the meeting with a "little" prayer. She keeps no written records and cautions the spiritual director to recite ten "Jesus Prayers" before saying anything or interrupting. She lets the spiritual friend know the session is nearly ending by saying "we'll have to stop in a few minutes," knowing that the person will now speak about the most significant material. She still stops the session at the appropriate time by saying, "Let's start with that next time." She keeps reminding the spiritual friend to talk about herself ("This is your time."), keeping on track with "what do you want me as your director to do for you? and What do you want

Christ to do for you?" or "Tell me about your work, your family, your friends, your health, your Christian community, what you do for fun." She knows that sometimes, what is being said is a confession, and she names it. She tries to help spiritual friends discern the "next right thing" similar to Mr. Dick in David Copperfield. sharing humor, tears, modeling Jesus as a spiritual director. Guenther compares the spiritual director to a midwife, waiting, like a ministry of presence amid the rocks, a hand to be held in the prevailing fear of labor, naming transitions. She identifies the process with the shedding of the skin of a snake, a skin which had to be formed to grow but no longer is useful. She describes a spiritual director as encouraging like a coach, celebrating new life.

Guenther spends her last chapter talking about women as spiritual directors and the gifts they may have to offer and the special concerns of women seeking spiritual direction. I love some of her feminine approaches, "If Priscilla had written our epistles instead of Paul, I suspect there would have been more about Incarnation and relatively little about circumcision." This was meaningful to me as I have been reading Guenther's book on a trip to the Greek islands and thought so much about Priscilla when we were at Ephesus, as she had moved there from Rome when the Jews were thrown out of Rome. She became a big supporter of Paul. Some have said that she might have written Hebrews. I will reread Hebrews and see if that might be true.

Margaret Guenther II

"Do not neglect to show hospitality to strangers, for by doing that some have entertained angels without knowing it."

–Hebrews 13:2

This is another quote from the beginning of Margaret Guenther's book, *Holy Listening: The Art of Spiritual Direction*. It had been on my bookshelf, half read for some time. I think I bought it around 20 years ago in Washington DC at the National Cathedral Museum Bookstore, attracted to its cover of the newborn by one of my favorite artists, Georges de La Tour.

I am guessing that Guenther picked this "work of art" because of the two women, one woman not speaking with a gently raised hand, almost like giving a blessing or in adoration, and the other woman looking intently at her sleeping newborn tightly wrapped like a gift or package. What an image for spiritual direction! I had been going for spiritual direction for many years, but it seems that the seed for me to do spiritual direction was planted in my heart and soul so very long ago before it germinated. As people started coming and visiting with me, I realized they were seeking spiritual direction, but they were not calling it that.

I decided I needed to take a course in spiritual direction on line from CDSP (Church Divinity School of the Pacific) about short term spiritual direction to feel out the waters. I kept moving in that "direction" and then five years later this course was affirmed when I spent two years in the Spiritual Direction Study at Kanuga with the Haden Institute. So, my energy was very high with Guenther's cover selection over twenty years ago, but it took this long to be affirmed!

Our God is a patient God and never gives up on a call.

Margaret Guenther III

"Lighten up" (don't) turn prayer into a work but listen for God and let oneself be surprised."

–Margaret Guenther, *Holy Listening: The Art of Spiritual Direction*. Cowley, 1992.

Again, Margaret Guenther's book, *Holy Listening: The Art of Spiritual Direction*, in my experience, remains one of the best practical handbooks for spiritual direction. She cautions us about setting up a rigid rule of life where Jesus is kept in a prison, and we only visit him at certain times. Jesus always likes to surprise us and have freedom to work in our lives in between the times we try to connect with him.

Guenther reminds us that the director's job is to be a guide, a midwife, to birth, to help bring forth knowledge that is already present in those coming for direction, where the therapist might spend more time analyzing.

The director needs to let herself be known in her own vulnerability and limitations as he or she encourages play (prayer), asks questions like "Could you say a little more about that? Can you give me an example of what you mean by...?"

The spiritual director should help the directee to live the questions, to keep peering into the empty tomb.

The director can encourage the directee to keep a log of her schedule to find times to pray, invite the directee to read psalms, or a gospel all the way through.

Guenther also reminds the director to keep that inner alarm that rings when we find ourselves becoming overly curious, taking sides or becoming over-invested emotionally in directees.

Guenther: Women

"If Priscilla of Thecla had written our epistles instead of Paul, I suggest there would have been a good deal about Incarnation and relatively little about circumcision!"

–Margaret Guenther, "Women and Spiritual Direction." *Holy Listening: The Art of Spiritual Direction*, Cowley, 1992.

Guenther reminds us to be sensitive to women's issues such as "not being deserving," women's tentative speech from fear of causing anger. She helped me realize my own fear of speaking out that I might say the wrong thing. She reminds us to be aware of the burden of repetitive menial work that women often do that is never done or finished that is part of their life style, doing work that so often is noticed only when neglected. She reminds us never to be condescending even when the story is not theologically sophisticated.

A spiritual director is called to help directees to trust their own voice. We are called to help both men and women to be comfortable with feminine imagery for God in prayer. She asks us to remind others of the brave women who anointed Jesus, and especially the story in Mark (14:3-9) of the woman with the alabaster jar when Jesus said, "Wherever the gospel is preached in the whole world, what she has done will be told in memory of her."

Guenther believes that the greatest sin in women is not pride but self-contempt often with an apparent absorption in triviality. She describes an icon for this is Virginia Woolf's Mrs. Dalloway, a day in the life of a high society woman in post-World War I London preparing for a party.

When we talk to women who may have been abused, Guenther suggests we ask the questions, "What do you want" and Where do you hurt?"

Guenther reminded me of times when I as well was verbally hurt by other colleagues but showed no anger, because it was not acceptable. I have allowed some other women and men repeatedly verbally to abuse me because I knew if I just stayed kind, it would change, and that there probably was something I had done wrong to deserve this action.

A question to ask when we sense verbal or sexual abuse is, "I sense you have been hurt a lot." When I perceive a special woundedness, I hope not to be afraid to ask the difficult questions, "Where was God when all this was happening to you? Where is God now? Do you feel angry at God?" I hope that eventually all of us will continue to see that God was there right beside us, suffering with us all along.

Lastly, Guenther writes about the danger of prematurity in prayers of forgiveness and reminds us to counsel those who come for direction to pray to want to be able to forgive--- someday.

Guenther: Holy Play

"Often what we call 'play' is competitive or compulsive, because the aesthetic dimension of true play, its holy uselessness, goes against our grain."

–Margaret Guenther, *Holy Listening: The Art of Spiritual Direction.* Cowley, 1992.

Holy uselessness. What a grand term for those of us who are driven. When I think of holy play, I think of just sitting, not reading or knitting, or thinking about my to do list, just sitting. (Some friends this morning reminded me that they did not want to be on my to do list.) Holy listening, holy uselessness can be just looking outside my window watching a breeze come and go and change my horizon. Many find that holy uselessness as they look out over bodies of water or mountains that call to us as icons to see through them or perhaps hear through them a connection to God. Nature changes the synapses, the pathways in our brains. Nature slows down the cerebral traffic.

Others find holy uselessness listening to music or playing an instrument. Instead of light waves we experience sound waves like soft free-floating harmonic speed bumps slowing down the traffic jam in our head to 2 to 5 miles an hour.

Sitting down on the floor with a young child can be holy uselessness as you try to keep up with them and follow their lead. Here we can become connected so easily to the Christ child in another and connect to the Christ child in each of us. At your next family dinner, volunteer to sit at the youth or children's table and just listen. You will find a whole new world, and it will be much more fun.

We usually do not put find holy uselessness on our to do list. The best part of holy playtime is that we can follow this spiritual practice anywhere, any time. It can change our life.

Guenther: Women as Listeners

"Again, and again I am struck by the number of women-of all ages, levels of education, and professional experience-who are drawn to some kind of listening ministry."

–Margaret Guenther, "Women and Spiritual Direction." *Holy Listening: The Art of Spiritual Direction,* Cowley, 1992.

I immediately felt an aha moment when Guenther writes that women in general are often called to a "listening ministry." This is where the introvert in me has felt called for so many years, perhaps since birth, and I have struggled because the role of deacons (to which I also hear a call) has been promoted as an active doing ministry out in the world, bringing the world to the church and the church to the world. And yet, can you not be bringing the world to the church one person as a time in pastoral care, sitting down and hearing the story of a person who comes to our weekly food pantry, listening as a spiritual director, being a facilitator of Mourner's Path, a ministry to the grieving, a ministry to the dying, visiting the sick in the world? In fact, Guenther speaks about our finding our most receptive spiritual friends among those who have been made outcasts by our society, like the Samaritan woman Jesus met at the well in John (4:5-42), those who live "at the economic, social or ecclesiastical edges." I don't regularly get this affirmation from outside of me, but I feel that affirmation inside of me. I think I still too often care too much what the outside world thinks.

Guenther counsels us not to do spiritual direction at home. I know many others agree. She lived in New York City where I think this would be more difficult. However, as I have mobility issues, my home and particularly in my living room surrounded by windows has more often become the set aside sacred place to meet that has been working well, but I am careful about having someone else in the house with me as well as other ethical issues. I never meet someone I do not know for the first time at my home, but with few exceptions, I have known for years the people who come for direction.

Three Days with Parker Palmer

During the Easter Season

Parker Palmer: Let Your Life Speak

"A leader is someone with the power to project either shadow or light onto some part of the world and onto the lives of the people who dwell there. A leader shapes the ethos in which others must live, an ethos as light-filled as heaven or as shadowy as hell."

–Parker Palmer, "Shadows and Spirituality." *Let your Life Speak: Listening for the Voice of Vocation,* Jossey-Bass, 2000.

I learned about Parker Palmer when I attended a College of Preachers conference just for deacons at the National Cathedral led by the bishop of Maryland, Robert Ihloff. We spent the whole week learning to preach and studying Palmer's book about vocation. Parker Palmer told us about what causes leaders to fail. We cast shadow rather than light when we fail to go on an inner journey and have insecurity about our identity and worth. Our identity becomes dependent on performing. When we are insecure about our own identity we create situations that deprive others of their identity or develop settings where others are required to build up our own needs. We create titles that place us above others. We call others by their first name while we must be addressed by our last name or title. Leaders fail when they see the universe as a hostile battlefield. We see the world as either allies or enemies where we must be highly competitive or we will lose. Palmer's third image of why leaders fail is functional atheism, a term he may have coined. We believe that the ultimate responsibility for everything rests with us. The fourth shadow within a leader that leads to failure is fear, fear of chaos. This fear leads to a rigidity of rules and procedures. We forget that creativity is born out of chaos. Finally, Parker sees leaders fail when they deny death. They keep resuscitating programs that are no longer alive, putting them on life support.

I can identify with all of these shadows of leadership. Do these shadows speak to you as well?

Parker Palmer: Trees

"I used to take trees for granted. But these days I know that sitting in their presence for a while will leave me refreshed and renewed. I wonder if trees photosynthesize the soul as well as sunlight? But most of all, I'm drawn to trees because of something W.S. Merwin says in this lovely poem — the way they slowly and quietly cycle through the seasons 'as though nothing had happened while our individual and collective lives whirl madly around them."

–Parker Palmer's response to W. S. Merwin's poem "Elegy for a Walnut Tree" on his weekly column on "Being with Krista Tippett," onbeing.org/author/parker-j-palmer, Wednesday, May 3, 2017.

I want to remember what Parker Palmer is telling us about the outdoors and trees especially. Could "trees photosynthesize the soul"? Being outside with trees does do something to my soul. Photosynthesis "is a process used by plants to convert light energy into chemical energy (sugar from carbon dioxide and water) that later is released to fuel the plant's activities and releases oxygen as a waste product." Plants are like transformers, changing one form of energy into another, changing light energy into chemical energy. Being outside in a forest does transform and quiet my soul. The busyness of my mind, the committee in my head, my to do list, no longer are managing my mind. I am grounded to the ground. I get out of my head into my body. I see a world greater than myself, a power at work greater than myself. As I keep returning to the forest I see how the trees do quietly "cycle through the seasons." The trees are a constant icon reminding us that we are to be the "steady bow" that Kahil Gibran writes about in *The Prophet* in his chapter on being a parent. We are indeed all parents caring for this earth that in turn also parent's us, cares for us.

My father was a forester who for so many Saturdays took people out to plant more trees. Often, we would drive by the pine forest to see how they were growing. This made some synapse change in my cells so that I always had difficulty seeing a tree cut down. This poem is especially meaningful to me today since two large trees in my neighbor's yard were uprooted last week just outside my window. Yesterday men with chain saws took the trees away. I grieve their absence. It helps to remember that our son and his wife had to cut down a tree that was dying adjacent to where they are building a house. They honored the tree by using the wood to make a mantle over their fireplace.

I look forward to hearing from you about what you have learned from trees and how you honor trees.

Parker Palmer: Seeking Sanctuary in Our Own Sacred Spaces

"Sanctuary is wherever I find safe space to regain my bearings, reclaim my soul, heal my wounds, and return to the world as a wounded healer. It's not merely about finding shelter from the storm: it's about spiritual survival. Today, seeking sanctuary is no more optional for me than church attendance was as a child."

–Parker Palmer, "Seeking Sanctuary in Our Own Sacred Spaces." *On Being with Krista Tippett,* September 14, 2016.

Our news is full of churches, towns, cities who are providing sanctuary to undocumented immigrants who now face possible deportation, dreamers, many who have been working and living and raising families in our country for years. They sought a better life for themselves and their families and now fear losing all that is sacred to them.

Many who come to spiritual directors are also seeking a sanctuary for their sacred spaces, a spiritual life that once had been vibrant but now may seem lost. They had decided to live and follow a road less traveled, but they have come to a spiritual fork in the road or perhaps a dead end. They fear they have lost the spiritual life they once had. They are now on a path that seems undocumented. Our ministry as spiritual friends is to be a sanctuary for the soul of those who seek our trust and guidance, especially at times when they feel isolated from their God connection. It can be a lonely time. We must treat as sacred this precious part of all people, that presence of God within each of us that we can sometimes obviously see but is blind to them or others. We must never lose sight of the privilege or the awesomeness of being asked to care for the soul of another, especially at a vulnerable time.

This is a sacred trust, a rare chance to make a difference, just as our churches in years past and years to come have been a place of sanctuary. I am told that the red doors of some of our churches are an ancient sign of sanctuary within. When we meet with a spiritual friend, may we imagine that we are sitting together just within the sanctuary of red doors.

We also are called to relate to other seekers in the world who need a sanctuary at this time of their life, in prayer and in person, remembering that we all are seekers and often are on an undocumented, uncharted path. Our hope is that we will have courage to stand, sit, sleep, work, eat, and pray beside all we need sanctuary within the red doors of our churches and our minds and our hearts.

Peterson: Prayer

"I began to comprehend the obvious that the central and shaping language of the church's life has always been its prayer language. Out of that recognition a conviction grew: that my primary educational task as pastor was to teach people to pray."

–Eugene Peterson, "What is my Educational Task?" *The Contemplative Pastor: Returning to the Art of Spiritual Direction*, Eerdmans, 1993.

The well-known author of the popular modern Bible translation, *The Message*, reveals his interpretation of the most important ministry of a pastor is being a spiritual director, teaching others how to pray. He is not downgrading teaching about faith or biblical writings or the history of God's people, but calls pastors to be spiritual directors, returning to the wisdom of ancient spiritual leaders who spent time training people to connect to God and God's love in various forms of prayer. He introduces people to making friends with our ancient forebearers, beginning with Gregory of Nyssa and Teresa of Avila, learning the language of intimacy, love, and relationship.

Peterson reminds us of two great mystical traditions of prayer, kataphatic and apophatic, one praying with our eyes open, the second praying with our eyes shut. The kataphatic prayer uses icons, symbols, ritual, incense, the creation as a way to the Creator. Apophatic prayer calls for emptiness with the mind emptied of thoughts and images until there is silence and the nearness of God. Both ways can be mixed and will be meaningful in our lives at different times. This former professor of spiritual theology, however, reminds us that the Psalms were written by people of God with their eyes open.

Difference Between Therapy and Spiritual Direction

"Converted anxiety is hope. Anxiety is dreadful expectation; hope is expectant desire. They are like cousins to each other. Pray for the conversion of your fretful anxiety into promising hope. If you are anxious just now, you are almost already hopeful."

–Br. Curtis Almquist, SSJE, from "Brother, Give Us a Word," a daily email sent to friends and followers of the Society of Saint John the Evangelist, a religious order for men in the Episcopal/Anglican Church. www.ssje.org

There is sometimes confusion between the ministries of a therapist and a spiritual director. We learn early in spiritual direction training that a therapist helps people deal with life on life's terms.

A spiritual director is a caretaker of the soul, one's connection to God. Sometimes helping people realize their connection to God can help them deal with life on life's terms, and often learning to live with life can reconnect us to God, but it can be very different. Becoming the person God created us to be, living a connected life can sometimes make life even more difficult, more challenging.

A spiritual director will listen to what is going on in a person's life, but he or she is looking for the God connection at every pause. A therapist will be looking at every pause for ways to lead the person to find a solution or way to deal with the pain they are knowing. A spiritual director focuses on one thing, seeing God at work in that person's life.

My favorite part of being a pediatric radiologist was caring for babies. When I meet with someone, I like to image their soul as a newborn they have offered over to me for a brief time to be cared for and nurtured and then gently returned to them wrapped in a warm blanket and resting and smiling at peace as they leave.

McQuiston: Finding Time

"That's when I stumbled across a quote from Rabbi Harold Kushner: 'for the religious mind and soul, the issue has never been the existence of God but the importance of God, the difference God makes in the way we live.'"

–John McQuiston II, *Finding Time for the Timeless: Spirituality in the Workplace*. Skylight Paths, 2004.

Memphis lawyer, John McQuiston II, is best known for his modern translation of the Rule of Benedict, *Always we Begin Again*. This third book by the author is a collection of real-life examples of spiritual practices of forty-two people known to McQuiston from varied religious and ethnic backgrounds who try to bring their spirituality to their workplace. The quote above is from his story about a Memphis religious writer of a column called, "Faith Matters," or as he explains, "it is not Religion Matters or Church Matters or Christianity Matters, but Faith Matters." This became so meaningful for McQuiston that he has it taped to his keyboard so that every day he will remember that he is not writing about religion per say but writing about how God works in our lives.

A Jewish engineer makes a gratitude list each morning in his 30-minute drive to work. His office computer is programmed to ask him: "What are you thankful for today?" The founding of an accounting firm develops a "mental peace" each morning by walking to work. A Greek orthodox dentist wears a cross under his shirt so he can constantly feel God's presence. He frequently says the Jesus prayer and has icons in his office.

Interspersed are also five short essays by McQuiston of his own awareness of how spiritual practices increase the quality of the rest of his life, encouraging readers to find a practice that brings them joy as well.

There is also an annotated reading list as well as an excellent summary or menu at the end of the book of the different practices described. The book is like a visit to a five-star restaurant where we experience a little taste of spiritual practices from many modern and varied sources. We are then invited to make a selection to experience our own life changing diet.

Prayer and Temperament 1

The Myers-Briggs Type Indicator is based on Carl Jung's theory of psychological types or personality preferences in four areas:

Energy source. Introverts (I) get energy from inside of themselves while extroverts (E) get your energy from outside of themselves.

Information method. Sensing (S) people gather concrete data while intuition (N) people think of possibilities.

Decision making. Thinking (T) people make decisions on what is logical while feeling (F) people make decisions on relationships and what is of value.

World View. Judging (J) people deal with the world in a planned organized way looking for closure when there is a problem while Perceiving (P) people are more flexible, spontaneous, keeping options open, and when there is a problem they keep gathering in data.

–Chester Michael, Marie Norrisey, *Prayer and Temperament: Different Prayer Forms for Different Personality Types.* Open Door Inc., 1991.

The Myers-Briggs Indicator test has been so helpful to me in understanding myself, my family, and those I work with. The above is just a short very basic summary. There also are a multiple of books about it and tests you can use. When I talk to spiritual friends I suggest they connect to a group or therapist who uses the indicator. I remember how helpful it was for me in my medical practice. We soon learned that we needed all types in our group. We need J's who wanted closure in solving problems, but we also need P's who wanted us to look at all the possibilities before deciding an answer. We needed T's who wanted our group to look at what was logical, but we need F's who looked at what was of value. We needed partners who were I's in our practice who did not speak until they had processed an answer inside, but we needed E's who solved a problem by thinking outside and vocalizing their thought process. We needed S's who looked at concrete data, but we needed N's who looked at possibilities.

So, the indicator can help us to live life on life's terms personally and in community, but how does it help on our spiritual journey? More tomorrow.

Prayer and Temperament 2

The Myers-Briggs Type Indicator is based on Carl Jung's theory of psychological types or personality preferences in four areas:

Energy source. Introverts (I) get energy from inside of themselves while extroverts (E) get your energy from outside of themselves.

Information method. Sensing (S) people gather concrete data while intuition (N) people think of possibilities.

Decision making. Thinking (T) people make decisions on what is logical while feeling (F) people make decisions on relationships and what is of value.

World View. Judging (J) people deal with the world in a planned organized way looking for closure when there is a problem while Perceiving (P) people are more flexible, spontaneous, keeping options open, and when there is a problem they keep gathering in data.

–Chester Michael, Marie Norrisey, *Prayer and Temperament: Different Prayer Forms for Different Personality Types.* Open Door Inc., 1991.

Yesterday we talked about how knowing the Meyer-Briggs personality types can be helpful in living life on life's terms. The classic book, *Prayer and Temperament*, tells us how the Myers-Briggs test is helpful in our spiritual life, especially in deciding on a way to pray. Lectio Divina or Benedictine Prayer is suitable for all personality types.

Augustine Prayer especially emphasizes feeling and intuition so may be best for the NF temperament.

The basic temperament of SP may best respond to Franciscan or prayer used by St. Francis.

Those with a temperament in search of truth and competency and learning (NT) may best pray using the Thomastic or Dominican Spirituality of Thomas Aquinas.

The Spiritual Exercises of St. Ignatius are most easily understood by the SJ temperament, but NT and NF temperaments also may find it a rewarding form of prayer.

Ignatian prayer projects us into a scene while Augustinian Prayer transposes the words of the Bible so that the Bible is speaking directly to us.

Those practicing Franciscan Prayer (SP) must be free and able to go wherever the Spirit moves them. Their prayer leads to action and their action is prayer. They cannot tolerate long periods of silence.

Those who would best practice Thomastic Prayer (NT) are logical and orderly and thirst for truth and address prayer like a scientific project or mystery.

God's Presence, Mystics

But the fruit of the Spirit is "love, joy, peace, forbearance, kindness, goodness, faithfulness, gentleness, and self-control. Against such things there is no law."

–Galatians 5:22-23

.

I recently met with an amazing group of people searching for God in their lives. Several questions were asked: "How do you know you are in relationship with God? How do you know God's presence? How do you know God is speaking to you?

I have always been skeptical of people who tell me, "This is what God told me to do." I do not know the voice of God until after something has happened, never before.

However, I have learned that I may be doing God's will if I feel the presence of the fruit of the Spirit: "love, joy, peace, forbearance, kindness, goodness, faithfulness, gentleness, and self-control."

We also can learn from the experience of others who were deeply aware of the presence of God. They are called the Christian mystics. Richard Rolle, the 14th century English mystic, describes being in relationship with God when he feels a physical warmth in his body, when he has an awareness of God's sweetness, and when he experiences a heavenly music as he chants the psalms. I know that indeed music touches our soul, that the sweetness and warmth Rolle feels may be from one of the fruit of the Spirit.

I have heard others say they have a gut feeling when they think they are doing God's will. Another common experience of the presence of

God happens when we are in Nature where we feel the presence of something greater than ourselves. Others also learn more about the presence of God when they become ill or lonely or are suffering or dying.

Experience tells me that people of the feeling (F) type in the Myers-Briggs personality indicator may be more inclined to develop this relationship experience with the Divine, but I also know that thinking (T) people can find this experience through logic and truth in research and reading.

–Ursula King, *Christians Mystics: Their Lives and Legacies Throughout the Ages.* HiddenSpring, 2001.

The Plural Me

"If I respect the plurality in myself, and no longer see my jealous self as the whole and greed and sloth is an opportunity to lift out of the waters of unconsciousness a tiny piece of submerged land of me, then I have gained the distance I need to observe it, listen to it, and let it acquaint me with a piece of my own lost history."

–Elizabeth O'Connor, *Our Many Selves: A Handbook for Self-Discovery.* Harper, 1971.

O'Connor's book was one of the first I read in trying to understand why I do the things I do, trying to find out what was underneath the surface or behind the mask I was wearing. Her classic writing gives us tools about how to become the person God created us to be. She teaches us about the many parts of ourselves and how God uses every part of us to connect to God.

Those parts of ourselves that block us from the Spirit are also pathways back to an even richer relationship to the God or Spirit within us. Christians would tell us that the life of Mary Magdalene is our scriptural example. Whatever her seven demons were, they led her to Christ and a new relationship with God and a new life. The recovery community would say that the recovering alcoholic or addict is led back to the God of his understanding in his journey to recovery. The Jungians would tell us that a recognition of the shadow or unloved or unaccepted part of us can become our hidden treasure or gold.

O'Connor presents a series of practical exercises she developed from years of group work at The Church of The Saviour in Washington, D. C.

to find these many parts of ourselves leading us to the God within and reaching out to the God in others.

Wolfe: Modified Prayer of St. Francis

We recently talked about the classic book about personality type and prayer styles, *Prayer and Temperament: Different Prayer Forms for Different Personality Types* by Monsignor Chester P Michael and Marie C Norrisey. The book is based on the Myers-Briggs Type Indicator Assessment and writes about five types of personal prayer developed over the centuries. If yours is the type Augustinian (Intuition, Feeling NF) where it is most meaningful that scripture or a message is written or speaks **directly** to you, this modification of the Prayer of St. Francis may speak to you. In this prayer adapted by spiritual director, Jane Wolfe, God, Jesus, the Holy Spirit is praying, speaking directly to you. Jane's premise is that we can take any petition and make it listening, thanksgiving, and praise, whatever we wish.

On the other hand, the more traditional version of the Prayer of St. Francis may be meaningful to you where **you** are praying directly to God. So, I have included it as well.

PRAYER OF ST. FRANCIS

Lord, make me an instrument of Your peace.

Where there is hatred, let me sow love;

where there is injury, pardon;

where there is doubt, faith;

where there is despair, hope;

where there is darkness, light;

and where there is sadness, joy.

O, Divine Master,

grant that I may not so much seek

to be consoled as to console;

to be understood as to understand;

to be loved as to love;

for it is in giving that we receive;

it is in pardoning that we are pardoned;

and it is in dying that we are born to eternal life.

—Book of Common Prayer

Use as a Monthly reading especially in Advent or Lent. Read one line a day for two days as if God/Christ/Holy Spirit/your Higher Power is saying this to you. Begin again with first day of each month.

1. I am the instrument of your peace.

2. Where there is hatred, I sow love.

3. Where there is injury, I pardon.

4. Where there is discord, I bring union.

5. Where there is doubt, I give faith.

6. Where there is despair, I bring hope.

7. Where there is darkness, I bring light.

8. Where there is sadness, I bring joy.

9. I console you.

10. I understand you.

11. I love you.

12. I give myself to you.

13. I pardon you.

14. I die for you.

15. I give you eternal life.

–Modified by Jane Lee Wolfe, "Spiritual Health and Fitness for the 21st Century." www.bogchapel.org

Earth Day

"For in him all things in heaven and on earth were created, things visible and invisible."

—Colossians 1:16a

The verse from Colossians is an ancient Christian hymn describing who Christ is. I also see it as a reminder of looking for the Christ in ourselves and others moment by moment. I know how difficult this is. Sometimes the Christ is so visible and sometimes invisible.

I think of Emily in the Thornton Wilder play, *Our Town*, who is allowed to return to earth for one day to Grover's Corners since her young untimely death at age twenty-six. She chooses her twelfth birthday and soon returns to her grave when she can no longer bear watching as the people she loves barely interact with each other and not appreciate the joy and wonder of each new day with each other and fail to see the Christ in each other.

I am writing on Earth Day and listening to music about the earth such as Beethoven's Sixth Pastoral Symphony as we travel from a reunion in Virginia to the gulf coast. This symphony always reminds me of the four years we lived in Iowa City. The music was the background for a visual production of the Iowa outdoors called *Iowa, A Place to Grow*, which always reminded us to bloom where we were planted and appreciate the beauty of the earth and the people of that state.

I remember the first Earth Day in 1970. It was the day my husband of six months left for Vietnam for a year. I was pregnant with our first child and feeling very sorry for myself. I spent the day watching the Earth Day celebration on our small black and white television and stripping the wax off the floor of our kitchen. I knew I had to transform the energy generated by Robert's leaving into something useful. I wish I was able to write that I went out and planted trees, but alas, my kitchen floor was as far as I got.

We are driving through a gentle rain and the car radio is now playing American composer, Alan Hovhaness' tribute to a beloved tree on his uncle's farm struck by lightning, "Under the Ancient Maple Tree." I wish I could say I participated in some marvelous events to care for and thank our earth and especially its trees on the other forty-eight Earth Days since, but I honestly cannot remember another Earth Day. Today the best I can do is enjoy the ride, give thanks for the rain, and give thanks for the bountiful green trees keeping us alive along Interstate 85.

I think of my father who was a forester who lead many hundreds of expeditions to plant pine seedlings. I remember on trips how he often would point out the tall grown trees that he had planted. I thank him now for his plantings many years later.

I have learned along the way that our environment, the outdoors, especially trees keep us grounded to the present moment. This is the present moment that I think Emily is talking about where we learn to appreciate each precious gift of time especially with those we love. My experience is that I most often begin to live in the present moment when I am outdoors and see the trees and plants and realize that there is something greater going on than the past and the future that I am concerned about.

CS Lewis and so many others and now Emily tell us that the present moment, not the past or the future, is where we meet and recognize God in ourselves, each other, and nature. This is the Creator, the God of Love.

Living Paradox

"The great paradox of life is that those who lose their lives will gain them. If we cling to our friends, we may lose them, but when we are non-possessive in our relationships, we will make many friends. When fame is what we seek and desire, it often vanishes as soon as we acquire it."

–Henri Nouwen, "April 30." *Bread for the Journey,* HarperOne, 1997.

Nouwen again lets us know a very real truth that we live and work with paradox, holding tensions. One of the best books I read during my work as a physician was John R. O'Neil's *The Paradox of Success: When Winning at Work Means Losing at Life. A Book of Renewal for Leaders.* O'Neil starts out telling us about how our excessive pride as leaders together with the seductive perks of power can become addictive with the wielding of power itself becoming more important than its goal. Power and need to control our own fate can take over, and control becomes the end rather than the means. The paradox of success is the promise of renewal as we can step back, especially in a retreat, and see where we have gotten into trouble. There are obstacles to stepping back such as our drive for perfection as our path becomes a prison and clocks tell us what we should be doing especially as we drive for the dead end of a substantial paycheck. O'Neil believes that any amount of time spent away from our usual productive round of activities is renewing as long as it is time spent in pursuit of some deep learning. For me it has been walking, being or sitting in nature, music, quiet, writing, talking and connecting with friends, visiting the sick, and some daily retreat which usually involves writing. He encourages us to become healed by pursuing some situation where we do not run the show as well as concentrating on relationships rather than goals or end results. Our difficulties stem from the very traits that make us winners. We will find gold in dark places.

He also shows a graph about success. We work hard to reach the top as we master our profession. We only stay there at the top briefly, for there is always someone else or many who will soon surpass us. O'Neil suggests that we stop to observe our situation as we approach the peak of a pursuit and consider starting all over again in a new career, beginning a new curve. That keeps us humble as we are back again on a learning curve where we are not the ones with all the answers. As we reach near the top of that career or undertaking, he again suggests we observe and consider starting all over again. As Benedictines might put it, "always we begin again."

Strangers, Angels, Firemen

"Do not neglect to show hospitality to strangers, for by doing that some have entertained angels without knowing it."

–Hebrews 13:2

Early in our medical careers as my husband and I were given the opportunity to help develop departments at Arkansas Children's Hospital, we were constantly recruiting out of town physicians looking at positions in our specialties several weekends a month. We also had three small children whom we wanted to be with especially on the weekends, so we usually took our children with us on tours of Little Rock and lunches in the afternoon. We often ate at a hotel restaurant that had an inside glass elevator and escalators, so when our children had enough recruitment entertainment at lunch, they entertained themselves by making several bird's eye view trips up and down the hotel.

I don't know if this term is still in fashion, but we would identify the visiting physicians to our children as "visiting firemen." The phrase is still a well-used part of our family vocabulary.

Many of these "visiting firemen" indeed were "angels unawares" as the King James Bible translates this verse from Hebrews. We had no idea how we would be able to work with those we were recruiting, but we took a leap of faith, and they changed and healed children's lives, and influenced us as well. They helped us put out fires when politics reared its ugly head in medicine. They taught us by their presence how grateful we were for them every day as we tried to solve and identify and change the course of children's diseases discussing and consulting with each other in community rather than making decisions by ourselves. Their presence and their wisdom changed me from an anxious person to a grateful person. They brought with them peace, one of the fruit of the Spirit in Galatians (5:22-23).

The greatest accumulation of strangers with whom I now meet weekly are at St. Mark's food pantry, but soon they as well are no longer strangers. Many indeed are angels. They ask for prayer, but they know how to pray so much better than we do. They have very little, but they share with others. Many bring their neighbors who cannot drive. Most repeatedly tell us stories about how blessed they are.

Perhaps, this is a sign of an angel, one who lives in gratitude.

I share with spiritual friends that I have learned most often from strangers that gratitude is a straight path to our soul, the God within us.

The Sea Is His

Venite
Come, let us sing to the Lord;
let us shout for joy to the Rock of our salvation.
Let us come before God's presence with thanksgiving;
and raise to the Lord a shout with psalms.
For the Lord is a great God;
you are great above all gods.
In your hand are the caverns of the earth;
and the heights of the hills are yours also.
The sea is yours, for you made it,
and your hands have molded the dry l, Band.
Come, let us bow down and bend the knee,
and kneel before the Lord our Maker.
For you are our God,
and we are the people of your pasture, and the sheep of your hand.
Oh, that today we would hearken to your voice!

–Psalm 95:1-7

He hurries in late with coffee in one hand and keys in another. "Sorry, about being late, trying to do too much, too much going on." I light our candle as a prayer to the Holy Spirit to be present. We sit in silence until his breathing becomes less labored. "When I am so busy, my world becomes all about me. I do not feel God's presence. I wish I knew how to slow down my life and better hear God working in my life," he finally says.

I tell him this story.

On our last visit to the Gulf of Mexico, my husband and I rose early whenever possible, sitting out on our balcony and waiting in the dark for the sun to rise. Usually the sun creeps up, a little pink, a little lighter, and then with a huge crash of light like the cymbals and tympani at the conclusion of a symphony. On a few days we become real beach bums, just sitting or looking out on the changing sea, waiting for the early morning fishermen: the osprey, the fishing boats, the surf fishermen with their accompanying blue heron waiting for the catch of the day. Soon come the dolphins and the pelicans swimming and flying and diving back and forth along the shoreline. We take in a world greater than of our own making.

The Venite from Morning Prayer from the *Book of Common Prayer* speaks to what happens more than we can express. One of our most famous theologians and philosophers who spent his lifetime trying to understand God, came and sat by the ocean for the very first time and wept uncontrollably as he experienced the vastness of God in the sea, more than he had ever imagined. Sitting by a body of water and observing new life as it emerges each day from under and above the sea, taking us into a world greater than of our own making can be more healing than drugs.

Is it possible for you to start the day, or stop during the day to sit by a body of water? For only a half hour, maybe during lunch or after dinner, stop and allow the rhythm of life on the river, or the sea, or the lake be moved to heal you.

Preacher, Sponsor, Spiritual Director

"The first time I was asked to give a lecture on preaching at the Festival of Homiletics, I wasn't sure what to say, so I asked my congregation. Almost all of them said they love that their preacher is so obviously preaching to herself and just allowing them to overhear it."

–Nadia Bolz-Weber, *Accidental Saints: Finding God in All the Wrong People.* Convergent Books, 2015.

Nadia Bolz-Weber is a very unconventional Lutheran pastor in Denver whose presence, writing, and preaching speak to so many of us because she is so aware of who she is and her struggle. I have found what her congregation is telling her about preaching is true for me in other disciplines as well. Everything I tell someone in a 12-step program as a friend or sponsor is actually what I need to hear in my recovery, pray every morning, make a gratitude list, do an inventory at night, make amends every day to the people I have harmed, remember I am powerless, keep doing the steps, keep going to meetings. This is also true as a spiritual director. What I say to a spiritual friend is also what I need to hear in order to keep my own connection to God, take time for silence, spend as much time outside where I may most realize the presence of God, look for Christ in myself, look for Christ in all I meet, be grounded in my body. When I forgot that I have need to hear all these things as well, in preaching, recovery, spiritual direction, I am in big trouble. I become like the Episcopal bishop in CS Lewis' *The Great Divorce* (chapter 5) who must leave heaven and return to hell because he is reading a paper to a theological society to enlighten them about how Jesus's teachings would have changed if he had lived longer.

Grace

"Like the unexpected call of a friend just when you need it most, grace arrives unannounced. A door opens. A path becomes clear. An answer presents itself. Grace is what it feels like to be touched by God."

–Bishop Steven Charleston, Facebook Post.

I stand waiting to walk out and read the gospel as we sing the hymn before the gospel, Dear Lord and Father of mankind. I glance at the last verse that the congregation will be singing just before the gospel reading. There, faintly written in pencil is the word, "softer," just before the beginning of the last line. It is my mother's distinctive handwriting. I had forgotten that my mother sang in the choir at her small Episcopal church in Virginia, and this must be a directive from the choirmaster. My mother has been dead for over nineteen years. We did not always understand each other, but when she died, I wanted to honor her in some way and decided to start using her personal hymnal prayer book in church. As you can see, her name has worn off the front cover, the gold cross will soon be gone, the red leather cover is now coming apart, particularly the back board of the spine of the book is gone. I have not repaired it because for some unknown reason what remains of this book just as she used it seems to be connecting me to her.

When I saw my mother's writing, I gasped and sent up a small prayer of thanksgiving. We had some very difficult times, but over the time since her death I have begun to feel healing. This morning, in this split second, I felt reconciled with my mother and was grateful for the life she gave me and her support.

Healing of family relationships takes time and constant prayer for that person and ourselves. Today I realize that prayer works. Attempting to connect to an estranged family member through something that family member treasures and we can share with them over time works. I know this sharing of what we have in common rather than our differences brings about healing in life as well as after death. My mother and I shared our love of the Episcopal Church and singing in particular. I almost felt my mother beside me.

Today I experience one more way that God's Grace continues to heal and care for us over time if we only put ourselves in position to receive.

Julian: Easter Follows Good Friday

"And all shall be well. And all shall be well. And all manner of things shall be exceeding well."

–Julian of Norwich.

January 13, 1967, on a rainy Friday night, fifty-one years ago, I was in a car accident when I was a junior in medical school that resulted in injuries that still plague my body today. I was driving a red Volkswagen and was hit by a drunk driver in a black Cadillac making a left-hand turn into a bar. I had to leave medical school for six months to recover partially from multiple extremity fractures. I never curse the mobility issues I still face today for one reason. I dropped back into the class where I met my husband of over forty-eight years. I do believe we never would have met if I had stayed in my first medical school class. I give thanks every day for his presence in my life. Any of you who know him will understand. This is when I first became conscious of Easters coming out of Good Fridays. I know that Eastering experiences had happen before in my life and in the lives of those I knew, but I did not recognize them.

Today I see resurrections daily in my life and others, the death of my grandfather leading me back to God and my grandfather's death leading me to stop smoking thirty-nine years ago. I see people in the grief recovery group we work with, Walking the Mourner's Path, changing the direction of their lives, reaching out to others in need because they know how difficult tragedy is to work through. They learn how to live on honoring the life and relationship of the one they loved who died.

I daily witness and see lived out these often-quoted words from the Revelations of the English mystic of the 14th century, Julian of Norwich: "And all shall be well."

Celtic Spirituality and Nature

"There is no creature on the earth
There is no life in the sea
But proclaims your goodness.
There is no bird on the wing
There is no star in the sky
There is nothing beneath the sun
But is full of your blessing.
Lighten my understanding
Of your presence all around O Christ
Kindle my will
     To be caring for Creation."

–Phillip Newell, "Wednesday Morning." *Celtic Prayers from Iona: The Heart of Celtic Spirituality*, Paulist Press, 1997.

The late Native American producer and musician, Jim Wilson, recorded the chirping sounds of crickets at regular and a slowed down speed which is said to match "the average life span of humans." In the slowed down version, the crickets seem to be singing alleluias (https://youtu.be/jk5gibBg-4g).

It is an impressive sound of praise from nature. No one else to my knowledge has been able to reproduce the sound, so it may be manipulated in some way, but nevertheless, I have listened to the recording so often that when I am outside in the night sky with the crickets, I hear an angelic chorus.

There is no question that the birds especially in the early morning seem to be singing a new oratorio each day to Creation as the sun comes up. The stars at night are like fireworks from millions of miles away reminding us of a spectacle beyond our comprehension. The waves at the ocean are like a percussion instrument that keeps us aware of a constant steady heartbeat of Creation, sometimes crashing like cymbals, sometimes soft like the ring of a triangle. I also hear from so many pet owners that they experience unconditional love first from their pets, especially dogs.

The love and praise of God is all around us, but especially in nature. Listen for it.

De Waal Trinity Connected

"If I am estranged from myself, then I am also estranged from others too. It is only as I am connected to my own core that I am connected to others."

–Esther De Waal, *Living with Contradiction: An Introduction to Benedictine Spirituality.* Morehouse, 1997.

Esther De Waal's writings embody the Celtic way of life. It is a life where we learn about ourselves in relationships to others, in relationships to ourselves, in relationships especially to Nature and the world outside and to daily life with almost constant prayer and connection to God and awareness of each precious moment. De Waal reminds us how easy it is to walk or drive rushing from one task to another without any awareness of the people we pass by in our paths. All too often instead of unconsciously sending love to them, we make unconscious judgements and labels as to who they are by their appearance or the clothes they wear.

I am indebted to her for one more book on Celtic spirituality, *The Celtic Way of Prayer: The Recovery of the Religious Imagination.* I am re-reading her chapter today on Celtic prayers about the Trinity as we prepare for Trinity Sunday. She reminds us of the Celtic tradition of placing three drops of water immediately on an infant's forehead after birth to symbolize the child's connection to the Trinity which is now indwelling in the infant.

The Trinity is a natural part of the daily songs and prayers at work as well as with the changes in the seasons. The day of the Celtic life begins with splashing three handfuls of water on the face in the name of the

Trinity. The day ends as the embers of the household fire are spread evenly on the hearth in a circle divided into three equal sections with a peat laid between each, called the Hearth of the Three. A woman then closes her eyes, stretches out her hand and softly sings this prayer:

The sacred Three

To save,

To shield,

To surround,

The hearth,

The household,

This eve,

This night,

Oh! this eve,

This night,

    And every night,

Each single night.

Amen.

– Carmina Gadelica, I, "The Trinity." *The Celtic Way of Prayer*, Doubleday, 1997.

De Waal describes what she has learned from the Celtic Trinitarian tradition, "It allows me to be at ease with a mystery that no longer threatens but supports, refreshes, and strengthens me."

The Threeness and connectedness of the Trinity also reminds me of a prayer that is anonymous but is sometimes attributed to William Blake but sounds so Celtic:

I sought my God;
My God I could not see.
I sought my soul
My soul eluded me.
I sought my brother
And I found all three.

Paschal Candles and Light of Christ

"After the Baptism, a candle (which is lighted from the Paschal Candle) may be given to each of the newly baptized or to a godparent."

—Book of Common Prayer

As a smaller candle is lighted from the large white Paschal Candle after a child is baptized, I often am privileged to hand it to the parent or godparent receiving it and say, "The light of Christ." Indeed, the Paschal Candle is often called the Christ Candle or the Easter Candle. Parents are encouraged to light this smaller baptismal candle they are given on the anniversary of the child's baptism as a yearly reminder of the light of Christ in each of our hearts and minds.

We may think the light of Christ inside of us is small, but we are called, mandated to share that light, and one of the ways to share our light is to encourage one another. As Paul modelled in writing so many letters to others, we are also called to connect with others who are carrying that light. That is why we have spiritual friends or connect with a spiritual director.

When our light seems to dim, the others with light will lead us to the Paschal Candle where we will once again find our light, often even brighter. We light the Paschal Candle during the Easter season, at Baptisms, and at funerals, all times when we want to, and need to be reminded of the light of Christ in our hearts, in others, and in the world.

Each time I meet with someone for spiritual direction, I light a candle when they come in. This is a reminder to me of how we are sharing the light of Christ with each other. I know I learn more in listening and talking with someone than what I can impart to them. We meet to see and encourage the light of Christ in each other. We meet solely to care for each other's souls.

Silence, Secret Easter Garden

"What will your secret garden look like? The point is to begin to slow down your life and focus your attention. Listen and in the quiet you will hear the direction of your heart. The garden of silence is always there for us. Patiently waiting."

–Anne D. LeClaire, *Listening Below the Noise: The Transformative Power of Silence.* Harper Perennial, 2009.

The Secret Garden by the American-English author Frances Eliza Hodgson Burnett, who also wrote *Little Lord Fauntleroy* and *A Little Princess,* is still one of my favorite stories. *The Secret Garden* is a story about an unloved 10-year-old English girl who is sent to live with her grieving uncle in his remote country home after her parents die. Her unhappiness and aloneness as well as the heartache and isolation of those around her are healed when she begins to spend time caring for and restoring a secret garden on the grounds of the manor house on the bleak moors of Yorkshire. I have watched the 1993 British film with Maggie Smith with my daughter and granddaughter and am going to see the play with my granddaughter this weekend. This story resonates with the child within us, the creative part of us, the part we so easily abandon for more important things, the part that is a major connection to the divine within us. It is another story about how the sounds, the smell, the sights in nature can silence and calm the grownup wounded committee in our heads and can heal and transform our inner child. We all should have a secret garden, a place where we seem to be able to reconnect so much more easily with the God within ourselves and the divine within each other. It is a safe place where the presence of the Spirit is more easily felt, described in

Psalm 32:7: "You are a hiding-place for me; you preserve me from trouble; you surround me with glad cries of deliverance."

Talking about our secret garden, our hiding place, often a place of silence, can be an opening to the divine in spiritual direction.

Frederick Buechner, Patrick Murray, Carl Jung: Synchronicity

"I remember sitting parked by the roadside once, terribly depressed and afraid about my daughter's illness and what was going on in our family, when out of nowhere a car came along down the highway with a license plate that bore on it the one word out of all the words in the dictionary that I needed most to see exactly then. The word was TRUST... The owner of the car turned out to be, as I'd suspected, a trust officer in a bank, and not long ago he found out where I lived and one afternoon brought me the license plate itself, which sits propped up on a bookshelf in my house to this day. It is rusty around the edges and a little battered, and it is also as holy a relic as I have ever seen."

–Frederick Buechner, *Telling Secrets*. HarperOne, 1991.

Frederick Buechner so beautifully gives us this story about synchronicity, or coincidences, or serendipity. Many believe this is an occasion when the unconscious speaks to our consciousness. How this happens is a mystery that Jung and Patrick Murray describe as "a relationship between an inner psychic experience and outer physical event." A synchronicity is "a **meaningful coincidence** that contributes to one's sense of wholeness."

In spiritual direction, we talk about looking for times of synchronicity, the occurrence of meaningful coincidences, being aware of them and pondering them, not letting them just slip by. Patrick Murray calls these "moments of transformation, embracing us with a profound sense that life is ultimately purposeful."

We sense a holy connection. A friend happens to call just when we needed it. We turn on the radio and hear a musical piece that brings back pleasant memories of a time we heard the music when we were with a loved one or dear friend. We feel peace. There are moments like that every day if we just step out of our routine to be aware of them.

At our food pantry I usually stand in a certain place inside and talk to those coming by for food. Today we came a little late and there were people sitting outside already just waiting for their grocery bags after they had put in their order. For some reason I decided to go outside and greet people there. Suddenly I saw a friend I had worked with for thirty-three years who had lost her job. We hugged and she told me about her struggles finding another job. I saw courage and faith as I have never seen before. She had a plan and was not giving up, and she still felt very cared for by a loving God. For me, this was synchronicity that we saw each other and could support each other just for a few moments.

I will put this visit in the memory book of my imagination and hope to remember to be on the lookout each day for ways like this that the Holy calls us and offers to us an opportunity to share the Christ in each other.

–Patrick Murray, "Jung's Concept of Synchronicity." The Haden Institute, December 2002.

Promises and Fruit

12 Promises of AA

1. If we are painstaking about this phase of our development, we will be amazed before we are halfway through. 2. We are going to know a new freedom and a new happiness. 3. We will not regret the past nor wish to shut the door on it. 4. We will comprehend the word serenity, and we will know peace. 5. No matter how far down the scale we have gone, we will see how our experience can benefit others. 6. That feeling of uselessness and self-pity will disappear. 7. We will lose interest in selfish things and gain interest in our fellows. 8. Self-seeking will slip away. 9. Our whole attitude and outlook upon life will change. 10. Fear of people and of economic insecurity will leave us. 11. We will intuitively know how to handle situations which used to baffle us. 12. We will suddenly realize that God is doing for us what we could not do for ourselves.

–*Big Book of Alcoholics Anonymous*. Alcoholic Anonymous World Services Inc. 4th edition, 2001.

Do you see any similarity between the promises of a 12-step program and the nine fruit of the Spirit (Galatians 5: 22-23)? Paul writes that we know and feel we are connected to the Spirit, the God within us if the consequence, the fruit, of what we are doing produces "love, joy, peace, forbearance, kindness, goodness, faithfulness, gentleness, or self-control." The promises and the fruit of the Spirit are both guides, benchmarks telling us if we truly on the right track, if we are connected to the God of our understanding, the Christ, the Spirit within us. When two disciplines tell me a similar truth, I begin to believe and pay attention to this truth.

Praying in Color

"Here are some reasons to Pray in Color:
1) You want to pray but words escape you.
2) Sitting still and staying focused in prayer are a challenge.
3) Your body wants to be part of your prayer.
4) You want to just hang out with God but don't know how.
5) Listening to God feels like an impossible task.
6) Your mind wanders and your body complains.
7) You want a visual, concrete way to pray.
8) You Need a new way to pray."

–Sybil MacBeth, *Praying in Color: Drawing a New Path to God.* Paraclete Press, 2007.

Gifted speaker and retreat leader, Sybil MacBeth, takes our prayer life conceptually from the left to the right brain. This type of prayer is especially easy for doodlers. It can initially be painful to those who theoretically live out of their left brain, those who are more verbal, orderly, logical, analytical, methodical in thinking, but praying in color can take that person into a whole new world of prayer. Those who are more right brained, more creative, imaginative, artistic, will rejoice that they can find a new method of praying that validates who they are. Sybil offers a multitude of ways to use this kind of prayer, as intercessory prayer, as an advent prayer calendar, as a way to memorize scripture, as a way of meditative prayer around a word or phrase, as a method for lectio divina, as discernment, and many more. We start with a simple shape, put a name or word within it and pray as we add or decorate or expand or connect the figure. This is a recommended adventure in prayer to the logical person who is stuck and the artistic person whose prayer life seems dry and colorless.

Seeking Wisdom

Canticle: A Song of Pilgrimage
    "Before I ventured forth,
even while I was very young, *
I sought wisdom openly in my prayer.
In the forecourts of the temple I asked for her, *
and I will seek her to the end.
From first blossom to early fruit, *
she has been the delight of my heart.
My foot has kept firmly to the true path, *
diligently from my youth have I pursued her.
I inclined my ear a little and received her; *
I found for myself much wisdom and became adept in her.
To the one who gives me wisdom will I give glory, *
for I have resolved to live according to her way.
From the beginning I gained courage from her, *
therefore I will not be forsaken.
In my inmost being I have been stirred to seek her, *
therefore have I gained a good possession.
As my reward the Almighty has given me the gift of language,*
and with it will I offer praise to God."

–Ecclesiasticus 51:13-16, 20b-22

"This Song of Pilgrimage from Ecclesiasticus" is one of the canticles offered for morning and evening prayer in Enriching our Worship 1, as one of the alternative canticles for the *Book of Common Prayer BCP*.

Christians inherited a pattern of daily prayer from the Jews, who set aside three daily times of prayer. More diligent Christians later took to heart the Psalm 119:164 verse that says, "seven times a day do I praise you," and by the Middle Ages monks developed a tradition of seven daily times of prayer: Matins before dawn and Lauds at daybreak which were combined into one service; then at sunrise, midmorning, noon and midafternoon were Prime, Terce, Sext, and None; Vespers came at sundown, and Compline at bedtime. This schedule was kept faithfully by monks and nuns in monasteries. Lay people could come when possible. In 1549 in the first English *Book of Common Prayer*, Archbishop Thomas Cranmer revised the structure so that ordinary people might also follow a prayer schedule and praise God at the beginning and end of each day now with just two services, Morning and Evening Prayer. The present 1979 *BCP* restored Noonday Prayers and Compline (A user's Guide to Morning Prayer and Baptism, Christopher Webber).

The theologian, writer, and founding editor of the Religion Department of *Publishers Weekly*, Phyllis Tickle, re-introduced a shorter version of daily observing the divine hours in a series of books, *The Divine Hours*, which many now follow. This is her pocket edition to carry easily with you. Her shorter versions of morning, noon, evening (vespers) and bedtime (compline) prayers, readings, and scripture are easier to observe than one would think and offer a frequent way to stop our work as we reconnect to God during the day and evening.

Brother Lawrence: Practicing the Presence

"Sometimes I think of myself as a block of stone before a sculptor, ready to be sculpted into a statue, presenting myself thus to God and I beg Him to form His perfect image in my soul and make me entirely like Himself."

–Brother Lawrence of the Resurrection, *The Practice of The Presence of God.* Image, 1977.

This very short book of a collection of four remembered conversations, sixteen letters, and a list of spiritual maxims of a French lay brother of a Discalced Carmelite in the sixteen hundreds is considered a spiritual classic about staying connected to God. Brother Lawrence initially worked at menial tasks in the kitchen for fifteen years and later in the shoe repair shop of the monastery. He lived a life of a constant conversation with God which brought to him the continually presence of God.

Brother Lawrence reminds me of Tevye in *Fiddler on the Roof.* Time for prayer was not different than any other time, since in essence he was in constant prayer. He believed the shortest way to God was a continual exercise of love by doing all things for the love of God. He believed that we do not need penance or skill at certain practices or deep theological knowledge to connect to God. We only need a heart devoted to God. He writes how God is often nearer when we are ill or weak than when we are in good health. He tells us to look especially for God in difficult times and instead of asking for relief from suffering, to pray for strength to suffer courageously. Brother Lawrence asks us to keep unceasingly knocking at God's door.

McQuiston: Always We Begin Again

"The first rule is simply this;
live this life
and do whatever is done,
in a spirit of Thanksgiving."

–John McQuiston, *Always We Begin Again: The Benedictine Way of Living*.
Morehouse, 2011.

I buy this book in bulk to give to those coming for spiritual direction.
My own copy is falling apart. It is pocket sized, so I can carry it around
with me throughout the day and leave by my bed at night. McQuiston is
a Memphis lawyer who has shaped and paraphrased the Rule of Benedict
into modern language. Its simplicity is its beauty. McQuiston's story of
how he was introduced into the Rule of Benedict is a reminder of how we
are constantly cared for by God. At his father's funeral, a priest friend of
the family gave him Ester de Waal's book, *Living with Contradictions:
Reflections on the Rule of St. Benedict*. This led him to Canterbury Cathedral
and a Benedictine experience and a major change in how he lived.

McQuiston distills a rule of life written for monks living in community
in the sixth century to an essential substance to help us in today's world
who do not live in a monastery find a balanced routine in an already too
busy schedule. I need to carry the book with me because I constantly
forget and get pulled off center and disconnected. I try to read the chapter
on humility every day, for "I have such great ideas." My rule of life
changes more often than I would like, but McQuiston keeps reminding
me how necessary it is to honor one, to stay connected to God and my
community, to stay thankful. A revelation for me in reading McQuiston's
book has been how close the Rule is incorporated in the 12 steps of

Alcoholics Anonymous. When two disciplines speak a truth, I try to take notice and realize this indeed may be a truth. The book also includes some meditative material and a sample rule of life. Sample it.

Ericson: Wounded Healers

"May our Lord Jesus Christ who walks on wounded feet, walk with you.
May our Lord Jesus Christ who serves with wounded hands, serve with
you.
May our Lord Jesus Christ who loves with a wounded heart, love with
you.
And may you see the face of Christ in everyone you meet.
And may the blessing of God the Father, God the Son,
and God the Holy Spirit be with you and remain with you always. Amen!"

–Borrowed from the Assisting Priest Bill Ericson, Holy Spirit Episcopal
Church, Gulf Shores, Alabama.

It takes some time to realize how our own difficulties or what Stuart
Hoke would call, our own darkness, are what make us able to know how
to minister to others as well as to connect to Christ. When our
woundedness is redeemed and worked through we are called to reach out
to others who also have been wounded. It usually is not helpful or at all
comforting to know this while we are being wounded or while the wounds
are still raw and open, but with time, our prayers can be that we make it
to the recovery room and move from victim to survivor and then
hopefully to healer.

The scars do not go away but are a reminder that we share these
wounds with Christ and the rest of a suffering world. I do eventually give
this prayer to spiritual friends who are seeking answers to their
unreasonable suffering over time, hoping they may be able to connect
their wounds to Christ. There are not answers, but hopefully we all can
see how we are not alone and how the God we are trying to connect to
also knows about suffering. God suffers with us and beside us and reaches

out to us through God's own presence and God's own wounds to offer connection and healing.

Day of Pentecost

Pentecost

"When the Day of Pentecost had come, the disciples were all together in one place. And suddenly from heaven there came a sound like the rush of a violent wind."

–Acts 2:1-2

"...he breathed on them and said to them, "Receive the Holy Spirit."

–John 20:22

Barbara Brown Taylor describes two versions of Pentecost, the gentle breeze in John as Jesus breathes into the few disciples fearfully gathered the night of his resurrection and the violent wind Pentecost described in Acts where the Holy Spirit goes all over the place with tongues of fire to over at least 100 people. The disciples with the gentle wind Pentecost are commissioned to take the Spirit out into the world. The ministry of the violent wind disciples is to seek and fan the Spirit already present in the world. Taylor challenges us that disciples in both Pentecost stories, those of a gentle breeze or the violent wind congregations are commissioned to find that Holy Spirit within them and others and take it out of their churches into the world.

The same is true of the Sprit, the Christ, within us. We are called to connect to that Spirit within us and then go out and connect to the Christ in others. If we don't we are like the disciples in John locked up in a dark room for fear of losing what we have. Only when we connect our Spirit to the Christ in others do we know that peace, joy, love that we are seeking. Our God also becomes larger as we become aware of the magnitude of God's creation and love.

Happy Pentecost.

–Barbara Brown Taylor, "God's Breath." *Journal for Preachers,* Pentecost, 2003.

Pentecost Continues

"When he had said this, he breathed on them and said to them, Receive the Holy Spirit."

–John 20:22

We are now in the season of Pentecost remembering, celebrating that the Spirit was given to us on the day of Pentecost. If you want to see what happened that day when the Spirit moved through a large room of people who do not have a clue what is happening, watch Bishop Michael Curry's sermon at the wedding of Prince Harry and Meghan Markle on the morning of Pentecost Eve. Usually the minister's words at a wedding are called a homily, a short sermon, but as one of the British commentators says, Curry's message is a true sermon, and it is all about love. He first describes love by reminding us that when two people fall in love, almost the whole world shows up as it does on that Saturday morning. That is how important love is.

Bishop Curry reminds us that love has the energy of fire, and his enthusiastic, passionate words are indeed like the Pentecost flames of fire running throughout St. George's Chapel at Windsor Castle. Bishop Curry is so filled with the Spirit that he has to keep holding on to his lectern to stay in place. His body language signals that he wants to move out and reach out more directly with the young couple and his congregation. As you watch people's faces, you can tell they have no idea what to do with him or his barnstorming message. They look mystified, amused, indignant, comical, questioning. Some look down at their program so others cannot see what they are thinking. Some glance at their neighbor to get a clue from them about what is happening. Some almost fall out of their chair! Some look at Curry as if they are mesmerized.

Perhaps the ones who seem to understand his message the most are indeed the royal wedding couple, especially Meghan who has a radiant smile with an occasional twinkle for the whole sermon.

Bishop Curry's presentation and delivery are not in the British style, but his message of love is true to his Anglican and African roots. He speaks out of his African American tradition from his ancestors in slavery and out of his training in an Episcopal tradition that Americans modified from immigrants from England who settled this country. Bishop Curry speaks his truth that comes from deep inside of him as all these traditions come together and kindle tongues of fire from the power of love that flame around the world.

Bishop Curry is our role model of what it is like to be filled with the Spirit. We have no choice but to speak the truth. Many people will not have a clue what we are saying, but everyone who hears us will be changed in some way. Bishop Curry also reminds us that the truth from God should always be about love, loving God, loving ourselves, and loving our neighbor. Period.

I have so enjoyed our journey together through Lent and Easter and hope to catch back up with you during Advent and Christmas and Epiphany.

Happy Pentecost Season.

About the Cover: A Myrrh Bearer

"But on the first day of the week, at early dawn, they came to the tomb, taking the spices that they had prepared."

–Luke 24:1

The icon on the cover of this book is from www.uncutmountainsupply.com, maker of Orthodox Christian iconography. This is an image of one of the myrrh bearers, one of the women taking spices to the empty tomb before dawn on an Easter morning. This is what I think Christ calls us to do. We are to bring what is costly to us, our intellect, our feelings, our intuitions, simply our presence, and look for the Christ in the world. We are called to look especially for Christ in those we think are physically and spiritually and mentally dead. We can only find Christ when we give of ourselves, freely, even when we sometimes know it may be dangerous.

We carry with us precious perfumes, costly spices. This is what each of our lives is made up of.

When we have been harmed or have sinned against our neighbor and cannot forgive or accept forgiveness, our life is closed up. We build walls, thick walls, tall walls. We do not want anyone to get in to see our own ugliness or we live in fear that we will be harmed again. We are like a jar filled with this precious oil closed tight. When we accept forgiveness and forgive, we lift up the top, and the bottle is opened.

Now myrrh is not the sweet pungent aroma like frankincense. It is earthy, woody, smoky. It is derived from a hardened tree sap. Myrrh has been used for thousands of years and is mentioned in the Bible over one hundred fifty times. It was used as a natural remedy, an antiseptic to treat wounds, and to purify the dead.

After this oil has been blessed, we might put some in a small dish and use it a healing service symbolically letting its aroma seep through the walls around our bodies, letting it purify the dead parts of ourselves, letting it heal our wounds and bring us back to a life in the resurrection.

But there is more. Next we are being asked now to go out into the world carrying within us or on us the precious myrrh that was shared with us. We are now myrrh bearers to heal each we see and meet in the world.

Joanna
joannaseibert.com
October 2018

CPSIA information can be obtained
at www.ICGtesting.com
Printed in the USA
FFHW010958030319
50767507-56182FF